THE
AGENTIC
BANK

Driss Temsamani's new book, The Agentic Bank, arrives at a critical moment for our industry. It is a must-read for financial services leaders seeking clarity amid chaos and hype, moving from experimentation to scalable transformation. The agentic bank is not a distant vision, it is already emerging. Leaders can help design it, or simply react to it.

Theodora Lau
American Banker Top 20 Most Influential Women in Fintech
Founder, Unconventional Ventures
Author of Banking on AI

The Agentic Bank is a masterclass in foresight. Driss Temsamani shows how AI agents will reshape finance from the inside out, making this an essential read for leaders preparing for tomorrow's economy.

Dominique Virchaux
President, Global Consumer Market & South America
Korn Ferry

Finance is shifting from platforms to intelligence, and Driss Temsamani captures that transformation with clarity and precision. The Agentic Bank provides a practical framework for how banks, treasurers, and policymakers can harness AI agents to drive speed, resilience, and trust at scale.

Rodrigo Luis Garcia
President, North America
Western Union

The AI hype in banking is deafening, but Driss Temsamani's The Agentic Bank cuts through the noise to provide executives with a clear roadmap for deploying agentic AI. Temsamani shows how intelligent systems and programmable assets create a foundation for trust, speed, and transformation in financial services.

Ron Shevlin
Chief Research Officer
Cornerstone Advisors

Over the last few decades, financial services evolved from branches to digital platforms. The next shift is from platforms to intelligence, and Driss Temsamani captures this transformation with clarity and precision. The Agentic Bank offers a practical framework for how institutions can harness AI agents to remain modern, resilient, and competitive.

Lex Sokolin
Managing Partner & Co-Founder
Generative Ventures

The Agentic Bank invites leaders to see banking not as a system to maintain, but as a living institution that thinks, acts, and learns. Driss Temsamani presents a compelling blueprint for how intelligent agents will transform decision-making, risk management, and client engagement in the next era of financial services.

Leandro Vilain
Partner, Financial Services
Oliver Wyman

Book design: Marko Markovic, 5mediadesign

ISBN (*Paperback*) 979–8–89965–561–6
ISBN (*Hardcover*) 979–8–90046–222–6

Staten House Publishing

www.TheAgenticBank.ai
Instagram: @theagenticbank
Youtube: @TheAgenticBank

HOW AI AND INTELLIGENT SYSTEMS ARE
REDEFINING FINANCE

THE
AGENTIC
BANK

DRISS
TEMSAMANI

Dedication

*To the builders, the bold, and the believers,
who see finance not just as a system to maintain
but as a platform for reimagination and
inclusion.*

*To those designing institutions that serve
everyone, not just more efficiently
but more equitably.*

*And to my family,
whose support and grounding
made this vision possible.*

CONTENTS

PREFACE

The financial industry is undergoing a transformation deeper than digitization, a shift that is redefining the very nature of institutional intelligence. We are witnessing the emergence of agentic systems, autonomous AI agents able to act with purpose, that don't just support financial operations but actively participate in them. They are not merely faster tools; they are a new class of collaborators that can think, reason, and act within the heart of an organization.

I wrote *The Agentic Bank* because this shift is not theoretical. It is already reshaping how value is created, how decisions are made, and how customers experience financial services. For those of us responsible for growth, strategy, and performance, the question is no longer whether AI will change the business; it is how to design for it, and how to do so in ways that accelerate performance, protect trust, and unlock new sources of value.

Banking has always been a story of interfaces. From the polished counters of grand branches to the glow of a smartphone screen, these touch-points have shaped how value is exchanged, trust is earned, and decisions are made. But today, a new chapter begins, not with a new channel, but with a new collaborator.

Imagine a treasury officer arriving in the office to find liquidity forecasts, market risk assessments, and regulatory alerts already analyzed and queued for action, not by a human analyst burning the midnight oil, but by an intelligent system working continuously in the background. This is not an abstract future; it is unfolding now in forward-thinking institutions.

This isn't a feature upgrade. It's a paradigm shift. We are moving from tools that wait for input to agents that anticipate needs and deliver outcomes—from dashboards that display information to intelligent systems that decide, act, and adapt in real time.

This book offers a strategic, structured, and practical framework for navigating this transformation. You will see how to design institutions where human talent and intelligent agents work together as seamless teams, delivering speed, insight, and resilience at a scale no single person or system could achieve alone. It is written for leaders ready to move beyond pilots and proof of concepts and into an era where intelligence is embedded in every function of the bank.

Welcome to the next chapter. Welcome to *The Agentic Bank*.

Driss Temsamani

Introduction

BEYOND PLATFORMS

W e are entering a moment unlike any other in the history of modern finance, not just a shift in technology, but a redefinition of what it means for an institution to think, decide, and act. The last great wave of innovation gave us platforms: powerful, scalable systems that unified products, data, and channels under one digital roof.

These platforms transformed the operational backbone of banking. They enabled self-service, digitized workflows, and connected front office to back. But they shared one fundamental assumption: that humans would remain the center of the decision-making process. People navigated dashboards. People initiated processes. People carried the burden of context, switching between systems, interpreting signals, synthesizing reports, and choosing actions.

That era is ending.

The next chapter in financial services is not about better tools; it's about new teammates. Agentic systems, autonomous, adaptive, and context-aware, don't just support humans; they collaborate with them. They understand institutional goals, interpret data in real time, learn from outcomes, and act within defined boundaries to move work forward.

Think of the shift this way: platforms were built for control. Agents are designed for cognition.

In the platform era, a relationship manager prepared for a client meeting by logging into a CRM, a portfolio system, a credit dashboard, and maybe a spreadsheet or two. They assembled the story manually, balances, exposures, recent transactions, and upcoming maturities. In the agentic era, the story arrives fully formed. An AI teammate synthesizes all relevant data, flags emerging risks, surfaces white-space opportunities, and even proposes a client agenda, all before the manager picks up the phone.

The difference isn't incremental. It's architectural. Platform thinking assumed linear workflows with human supervision. Agentic design assumes distributed reasoning across humans and machines, where both learn and adapt continuously.

This is not a technical adjustment. It is a strategic realignment. It forces us to reimagine the operating model of finance itself:

- What is the role of a human banker when the system understands context?
- How is risk governed when agents act in milliseconds across markets?
- Where is value created when knowledge flows are instantaneous, personalized, and predictive?

In an age where speed, precision, and trust determine competitive edge, the agentic model is not optional. It is inevitable.

This book is your blueprint. By the time you finish, you'll know how to design, build, and lead institutions where humans and intelligent systems operate as a single, cohesive team, faster, smarter, and more resilient than ever before.

You'll find no hype here. No overpromises. Just clarity, structure, and vision, grounded in the operational realities of today's banks and the strategic imperatives of tomorrow's economy.

If you are a banker navigating complexity, a policymaker shaping digital rules, a technologist architecting next-generation systems, or an investor wondering what future-ready institutions look like, this book is for you.

The platform era gave us scale.
The agentic era gives us intelligence.
Let's build what's next.

Chapter 1

A NEW FINANCIAL SPECIES

To understand how to build what's next, we must first be clear about what we're striving toward. For more than a century, financial institutions were designed for a world where humans made all the decisions, machines followed instructions, and infrastructure enforced process. For decades, innovation meant doing the same things, just faster, more securely, or on smaller screens.

That world has changed, quietly at first, and then all at once.

This is the rise of *agentic systems*. In these pages, we will call it what it is: a new institutional species. Built on programmable financial infrastructure, orchestrated by intelligent agents, and governed by intent, the Agentic Bank is defined not by where it operates, but by how it thinks and acts.

If your institution is still focused on systems and dashboards, it will struggle to compete in a world where clients expect *intelligent outcomes*. The competition is no longer just another bank across the street. It is a constellation of agentic systems, tuned to anticipate needs, personalize experiences, and execute decisions at scale.

Institutions built for human operators must be reimagined for autonomous collaborators. Those who do it first, and do it well, will shape the next generation of financial value creation.

The Pattern of Disruption

Banking has always been a story of interfaces. The next interface is *cognitive*.

Throughout history, financial services have evolved in response to technological revolutions, each a tipping point that redefined business, productivity, and human behavior.

In 1784, the invention of the mechanical loom signaled the beginning of the Industrial Revolution, introducing the age of mechanization. It transformed production and labor. Nearly two centuries later, in 1969, the introduction of the personal computer marked an inflection point that digitized office work and information processing. In 2007, the launch of the iPhone catalyzed the mobile-first era, embedding computing into our daily lives and enabling the rise of app-driven, real-time experiences.

Each epoch birthed new business models, platforms, and organizational behaviors. And now, in 2025, we stand at the edge of another monumental shift: the agentic era. *Generative AI* and autonomous AI agents represent a phase where intelligence, not just interface or data, becomes programmable. What began as machine learning predictions has matured into systems that can perceive, reason, and act, capabilities once reserved for humans.

This moment signals a fundamental change in how we partner with technology, moving beyond simply what it can do to what it can decide and execute on our behalf.

As Steve Jobs once remarked, "You can't connect the dots looking forward; you can only connect them looking backward." From loom to PC to smartphone, the pattern is clear. Agentic banking is not a question of *if*, but *when*. And like every major shift before it, this transformation builds on what came before while fundamentally redefining what comes next.

Each prior phase made banking more accessible, but all were designed around human operators.

Whether using a pen, terminal, or smartphone, the human initiated the action, interpreted the data, and approved the decision. The systems, no matter how advanced, remained passive.

Not this time. In this new phase, systems act, decide, and adapt, and that changes everything.

What Makes This Different

Unlike traditional systems that wait for human input, agentic systems observe, infer, and initiate. This shift demands a rethinking of infrastructure, roles, and trust.

In a traditional environment, a treasury manager might receive an alert, check multiple data points, consult with the risk team, and then execute a funding action. In an agentic environment, the system already understands the liquidity mandate, monitors macro conditions, and either proposes or directly executes the optimal action with compliance validation embedded at every step.

Perhaps the biggest differentiator is that agentic systems reframe the workflow itself. They operate continuously, not in batch cycles or limited user sessions, and they do so across domains. A liquidity agent, for example, reasons about funding needs, market volatility, risk appetite, and regulatory exposure, and then proposes action. When connected to a programmable substrate, it can execute that action in near real time.

In practical terms, this unlocks speed, scale, and personalization that legacy models simply cannot match. Clients want results, not reports:

"Preserve my capital, manage FX risk, and keep me ESG-compliant."

The institution that can transform that statement into continuous, real-time execution, transparently, securely, and without friction, will dominate not by product, but by intelligence.

That is the competitive edge of the agentic bank.

Why Now? The Urgent Imperative

The transformation to agentic banking is already underway. The forces accelerating it are structural, not cyclical, creating an urgent imperative for action. Today's institutions face:

Data explosion – Financial services are drowning in information: client behavior, risk signals, regulatory updates, ESG mandates, and real-time market dynamics. Human processing can no longer scale to match the pace or volume. What's needed is not more dashboards, but systems that interpret and act on data with minimal delay.

Shifting customer expectations – Clients, both retail and institutional, now expect services to be personalized, proactive, and instantaneous. The benchmark is no longer the last banking experience; it's the frictionless, tailored outcomes delivered by the best digital platforms anywhere. People don't want ten more features; they want one intelligent result.

Dynamic regulatory and compliance demands – Rules are evolving faster than manual oversight can handle. The solution is governance-by-design: systems where controls are embedded from the start, ensuring continuous transparency and auditable logic.

Fragmented competition – Advantage is now defined by speed and adaptability, not just balance sheets.

In short, agentic banking matters now because the gap between *decision* and *action* has become a liability. Closing that gap is the next frontier of institutional performance.

The agentic model is purpose-built for this. It reconfigures capability to perceive context, prioritize intelligently, and act within constraints.

- **In treasury**, agentic systems synthesize global inputs, align with strategic funding goals, simulate downstream effects, and propose, or execute, optimal decisions across counterparties and currencies. The result: enhanced strategic agility.

- **In client experience**, intelligence shifts from reactive to proactive. Agents learn individual behaviors and preferences, anticipate needs, and coordinate across products to deliver relevant, timely, and compliant outcomes. Personalization becomes proactive, not cosmetic.
- **In compliance and risk**, prevention replaces reaction. Instead of flagging exceptions after the fact, embedded logic monitors for deviations in real time and enforces institutional thresholds as a native function of process.

Why It Matters Now

This matters now because the cost of friction, in time, trust, and margin, has never been higher. Performance will no longer be driven by headcount or hardware, but by how intelligently an institution can act and how quickly it can learn.

The urgency is amplified by the shift toward a financial environment that is increasingly modular, programmable, and agent-compatible, favoring systems that coordinate across networks rather than dominate within silos.

Initiatives like the *Finternet* and regulated digital asset networks are pushing toward composable infrastructures, where money, identity, and contracts are represented as code and executed through logic, not paper. In these environments, agentic systems are not optional; they are a necessary capability to navigate complexity and deliver outcomes in real time.

Clients will not wait for legacy systems to catch up. They will route around them.

This reality is already visible in early agentic treasury pilots, programmable ESG investing, and tokenized asset orchestration. Every delay in rearchitecting for agentic systems cedes ground to more adaptive players, whether fintechs, ecosystem platforms, or digitally native financial institutions. In a world of intelligent systems, inertia is a competitive risk.

This book is written now because action is required now. For the first time in banking history, three essential conditions have converged:

- **Intelligence** – Agents can reason, remember, and act.
- **Infrastructure** – Smart contracts and APIs provide a programmable operational substrate.
- **Incentives** – Clients want intelligent outcomes, not more tools.

Institutions that recognize this convergence will define the operating standard for the next generation of finance. Agentic banking offers a path forward that is not just efficient, but transformative:

human-guided, AI-accelerated, and outcome-optimized.

Why it matters now is simple: The tools exist. The need is urgent. And the opportunity is real.

The Transformation Required

To embrace agentic banking, institutions must first abandon the illusion that incremental improvement is enough. The old model, layering new technologies onto legacy decision trees, cannot keep pace with environments defined by volatility, data saturation, and client expectations for instant responsiveness.

The agentic model delegates what slows us down, routine interpretation, cross-referencing systems, and execution under policy, to systems that can manage scale and complexity with precision.

We've seen this before in other industries. In logistics, global supply chains no longer rely on manual coordination. In digital advertising, autonomous bidding platforms make thousands of micro-decisions per second to match creative with audience. Financial services are next, but here, the stakes are higher and the systems far more complex.

To enable this shift, institutions must move beyond static systems into programmable architectures: modular, event-driven, API-connected environments that allow agents to reason and act across silos. And it starts with reimagining the institution, not just upgrading it.

Building toward an agentic model requires more than plugging AI into existing workflows. It demands a layered transformation, technological, cultural, and architectural. Financial institutions must invest not only in intelligent agents, but in agentic environments: composable, event-driven systems where agents can perceive context, interpret rules, and initiate coordinated action.

This is where programmable finance becomes essential. Agents interact with tokenized assets, smart contracts, dynamic APIs, and identity frameworks that authenticate intent across networks. Without this infrastructure, intelligence risks becoming insight without action.

In this context, agentic banking becomes the conductor of intelligent flows.

But with new capability comes new responsibility. Governance must be embedded from the outset. We need new metrics, new trust architectures, and new roles, not for managing agents, but for collaborating with them.

The potential is massive: faster treasury cycles, goal-driven personalization, and audit trails generated by design. All of this rests on enabling intelligent agents to operate safely, transparently, and under firm institutional guardrails.

Defining the shift means acknowledging a simple truth: the role of the financial institution is evolving from controller of processes to orchestrator of outcomes. That also means leadership must evolve, from optimizing current systems to designing for continuous, agent-led collaboration.

Leadership Shift

Since the urgency demands a fundamental shift, leaders must step up. Leading in this environment means embracing a new kind of leadership, one rooted in intent, orchestration, and systemic thinking.

This shift requires three core changes in how you lead:

From Command to Configuration – Instead of issuing instructions through rigid processes, you define goals, parameters, and policy constraints. The system interprets and acts. Your role becomes curatorial, configuring environments that drive intelligent action, not micromanaging every step.

From Centralization to Collaboration – Agentic systems thrive in modular, distributed architectures. Your teams must be cross-functional by design. Product, compliance, risk, and technology teams no longer hand off, they co-design. Governance becomes participatory, and iteration becomes continuous.

From Static to Adaptive KPIs – Traditional metrics often lag or oversimplify. In agentic systems, performance is real-time, contextual, and feedback-driven. New indicators must capture outcome quality, responsiveness, agent alignment, and the effectiveness of human oversight.

As intelligent agents handle execution, your strategic bandwidth expands. You can shift focus from troubleshooting to tuning, from escalation to evolution. As your institution's capacity to learn increases, so does its competitive resilience. What you design now, in architecture, policy, and human–machine interaction, becomes the operating logic of your future enterprise.

Your Role in Building the Future

What follows is for you, the executive, the builder, the orchestrator of institutional performance, and how to act on it starting today.

Whether you're a business line head, a chief digital officer, a compliance executive, or a product strategist, you are designing the future.

And as such, you must:
- Shift from workflows to behaviors.
- Launch not features, but intelligence.
- Redefine success as coordinated outcomes.

You must ask yourself:
- Can this process be represented by intent rather than by steps?
- Can this agent act autonomously while staying within governance boundaries?
- Can this interaction evolve in real time based on data, context, and feedback?

You're moving from managing tasks to orchestrating outcomes. That shift requires a different approach to how teams are structured, how systems are integrated, and how success is measured.

Agentic systems don't just unlock efficiency. They unlock growth. Those who understand this will lead the next phase of financial innovation. Those who don't will find themselves optimized for a world that no longer exists.

This book will support your transition, conceptually and structurally. Each chapter offers frameworks, patterns, and examples aligned with the strategic questions institutions must now answer:
- How do we define agent roles and boundaries?
- How do we design systems that balance autonomy with control?
- How do we build trust, not just between users and systems, but among systems themselves?

- How do we restructure teams, workflows, and governance for an agent-first model?

You'll see use cases across treasury, compliance, risk, ESG, and client experience. You'll learn how agentic systems integrate with programmable infrastructure, and how institutions can evolve from managing rules to encoding intent. The focus is not on technology alone, but on redesigning institutional behavior.

It's not enough to deploy agents. You must create environments where people trust, guide, and collaborate with them. That requires new skills, new confidence, and a clear understanding of where human judgment is most valuable.

The agentic bank demands a full-scale redesign, an intentional composition of what comes next, rather than a modification of what already exists.

And now you have this book to show you how to build it.

Let's begin.

Chapter 2

LISA'S WORLD, THE AGENTIC INSTITUTION IN ACTION

Setting the Scene: Lisa's Role & Environment

Lisa steps into the executive suite of a leading multinational institution, but she doesn't do it alone. By the time her ID badge grants her access, three agentic systems have already begun shaping her day: a treasury forecasting agent, a compliance sentinel, and a client intelligence orchestrator. These are not silent background tools; they are collaborators, autonomous and context-aware digital entities that anticipate her needs, flag anomalies, and proactively recommend actions.

As Global Head of Liquidity, Lisa operates in a world of extraordinary complexity and interdependence, overseeing trillions in flows across dozens of jurisdictions, currencies, and counterparties. A liquidity misstep in one region can ripple across the balance sheet within hours, triggering funding stress or regulatory scrutiny. Her job once meant navigating spreadsheets stacked like barricades, surviving late-night crisis calls, and manually triaging cash positions with incomplete data. Today, it is defined by orchestration. Lisa no longer asks, *"What's going wrong?"* She asks, *"What are my agents doing about it?"*

Her team has transformed alongside her role. Human specialists still provide governance, interpret nuance, and craft long-term strategy, but the tempo of their work has changed. Instead of firefighting yesterday's problems, they supervise a network of agents that detect stress early, adapt to live market signals, and continuously recalibrate forecasts, recommendations, and funding actions. The cadence of decision-making has shifted from episodic to continuous, from reactive to anticipatory.

Lisa's workspace reflects this evolution. She no longer toggles between fragmented dashboards or hunts through raw spreadsheets. Instead, she engages through a unified, conversational interface that speaks in natural language, surfaces insights in narrative form, and explains the rationale behind each recommendation. Every proposed action arrives with a reasoning trail, a confidence score, and references to the policies applied. She can override or escalate with a single command, knowing every action, whether agent-driven or human-directed, feeds back into the system's memory. This is not just a console. It is a command center for a distributed mesh of intelligent collaborators.

Here, trust is engineered into the workflow. Lisa can trace why a compliance sentinel flagged a suspicious flow in Hong Kong, or how the treasury forecasting agent adjusted its liquidity model in response to a sudden FX swing in Tokyo. Transparency is not a report generated after the fact; it is woven into every recommendation in real time. Her confidence in the system comes not from blind faith but from explainability and alignment, the trust scaffold that makes agentic collaboration credible at scale.

Most striking, perhaps, is how seamlessly the agents collaborate with one another. The client intelligence orchestrator may alert Lisa to a corporate client's deteriorating repayment posture. Within seconds, the treasury agent recalibrates liquidity exposure, while the compliance sentinel checks for cross-border risk triggers. Lisa doesn't see competing alerts; she sees a synthesized briefing, orchestrated across domains, showing her how the system itself is reasoning through the problem. The agents do not merely automate tasks; they compose intelligence across silos, something her old spreadsheets and dashboards could never achieve. For Lisa, this represents more than a change in tools. It is a change in how her institution thinks. She is not managing processes; she is shaping the behavior of an intelligent institution that perceives, reasons, and acts with her. In this world, leadership is no longer about having the best data at hand, but about designing the guardrails, governance, and intent that shape how intelligence itself is deployed.

A Day in Lisa's Agentic World

At 9:15 a.m., Lisa's treasury agents issue their first update, a prioritized, contextual summary: "Your projected funding cushion in Argentina has tightened due to unexpected outflows and pending settlement delays in Brazil. Recommended actions: 1) advance liquidity buffers from the regional hub; 2) alert FX hedging agent; 3) simulate 48-hour stress exposure."

This is not a static report, it is a living narrative, continuously updated as new signals flow in. The update arrives with a confidence level for each recommendation and a transparent reasoning trail showing how the system weighted regional outflows against historical seasonal patterns and recent counterpart behavior.

Lisa taps once to review simulated impact scenarios, dynamic models co-generated by agentic intelligence using real-time market feeds, behavioral modeling, and embedded policy constraints. The system proposes a ranked set of next steps, from the most conservative buffer move to a more aggressive hedging strategy, each tied to risk-adjusted return projections. Unlike the opaque models of the past, every recommendation is accompanied by a rationale that Lisa can interrogate, annotate, or share downstream with colleagues, regulators, or the board.

Historically, this type of analysis would have required hours of coordination among analysts, risk officers, compliance reviewers, and operations staff, often using inconsistent datasets and fragmented dashboards. Today, her agents pull from the institution's agentic memory, using retrieval-augmented generation (RAG) to surface the most relevant policies, counterparty exposures, and jurisdiction-specific rules. What once demanded laborious reconciliation now arrives in the form of decision-ready intelligence.

A second notification pings: the sovereign counterparty in question is approaching a risk threshold that had been pre-set by compliance agents. The system does not merely flag the issue; it prompts

Lisa to reroute exposure through a secondary clearing path. With a single command, her orchestration layer initiates the sequence: approval requests are routed to control functions, pre-validated transaction proposals are generated, and counterparties are notified.

Lisa's role is not to manage spreadsheets or approve isolated transactions, it is to supervise intelligence. She steps in when judgment is needed, but even then, the system provides insight, alternatives, and contextual overlays, ensuring she has the clearest possible view of consequences before committing. When she acts, her decisions feed back into the institutional memory, fine-tuning future responses.

What emerges is a treasury that no longer functions as a set of parallel teams or siloed processes but as a neural network, sensing, reasoning, and moving as one. Liquidity management has shifted from episodic decision-making to continuous alignment, with humans and agents working in a rhythm that feels less like oversight and more like orchestration.

Client Engagement: CX Agents at Work

By mid-morning, Lisa shifts her focus to a strategic review with one of the institution's most important clients. Well before she enters the room, her client experience agents have assembled a forward-facing intelligence summary: *"Client X is likely to pursue liquidity restructuring in Q3. Signals: portfolio reallocations, changes in counterparty hedging positions, and macro commentary from the CFO in their most recent earnings call."*

This briefing is not a product of any single dataset but of a composable intelligence mesh. Multisource signals, earnings transcripts, analyst call notes, transactional metadata, and even public sentiment indicators, are ingested and contextualized by LLMs fine-tuned on the institution's proprietary governance and compliance guardrails. The output is not simply predictive but explainable: each inference arrives with source citations, reasoning chains, and confidence levels, allowing Lisa to probe deeper when needed and ensuring that client-facing intelligence remains both transparent and defensible.

Beyond forecasting needs, Lisa's client experience (CX) agents have simulated multiple pathways for value creation. They propose tactical service enhancements: adjusting liquidity sweep thresholds in anticipation of volatility, bundling real-time FX execution with treasury optimization, and co-timing collateral release with market cycles to maximize capital efficiency. Each option is scored for impact and mapped against both regulatory constraints and the client's historical behaviors. From these simulations, the agents have auto-generated a tailored client proposal, complete with rationale, risk-benefit analysis, and a governance layer pre-reviewed by compliance, ensuring that no suggestion exceeds policy boundaries.

Before stepping into the meeting, Lisa engages her conversational interface to rehearse. The client co-pilot agent anticipates objections, role-plays possible counterarguments, and sharpens her responses. It draws on the client's prior negotiation history, stated strategic priorities, and jurisdictional sensitivities, ensuring that Lisa walks into the conversation with not just information, but foresight.

When the meeting begins, Lisa no longer relies solely on memory or paper notes. She co-navigates the session alongside her agents, surfacing data and insights on demand, contextualizing responses with precision, and adapting dynamically as the client's questions evolve. The interface operates as an explainability console, allowing Lisa to show *why* certain recommendations are being made, turning a potential black box into a shared reasoning process the client can trust.

The effect is tangible. The client no longer feels like they are negotiating with a single executive supported by static reports. They experience a partnership guided by intelligence, responsive, transparent, and deeply aligned to their needs. This is client engagement elevated, where agents do not just serve as tools, but as collaborators who know, think, and act with purpose.

Governance in Motion: Compliance Escalations

Just after lunch, Lisa's workflow is interrupted by a high-priority escalation. Her compliance agent surfaces a deviation in intraday transaction behavior from a cross-border affiliate, an anomaly that, while not immediately material, echoes a past pattern tied to sanctions evasion. The inference is not guesswork but the product of layered intelligence: temporal anomaly detection, behavioral clustering, and the institution's agentic memory, which recalls and compares past events across jurisdictions.

The alert does not arrive as a flashing red box or an indecipherable code. It comes as a narrative: *"Detected transaction path exhibits a 72% similarity to prior flagged behavior in 2023, originating from the EMEA hub. Recommended action: conditional hold. Routed to human compliance lead for review."* In plain language, Lisa can understand what was detected, why it matters, and what the next steps could be.

What once required frantic coordination is now seamless. Lisa does not need to assemble an ad hoc meeting or chase signatures across departments. The governance mesh is already in motion. The compliance agent has alerted the responsible officer, triggered a live scan of all transactions linked to the entity, and drafted a regulatory incident report for immediate use should escalation be necessary. Legal, risk, and operations stakeholders are automatically looped in, each provided with tailored context relevant to their mandate.

More importantly, the system interprets the likely downstream impacts: reputational exposure, potential fines, liquidity disruptions, and client service implications. It does not stop at detection; it proposes mitigations, rerouting exposure, tightening transaction monitoring, or temporarily adjusting risk thresholds, all while flagging the decision points where human judgment is required. Lisa can override, approve, or request further analysis, each action logged immutably in the audit trail.

Governance here is not sacrificed for speed, it is strengthened by it. Instead of being a post-event bottleneck, compliance becomes a real-time capability, ambient across transactions and adaptive to emerging risks. This turns regulatory alignment from a defensive exercise into a source of strategic advantage. In Lisa's world, trust is not an afterthought; it is engineered into the system, continuously reinforced through explainability, accountability, and speed.

Volatility Response: Stress Testing in Real Time

At 3:22 p.m., the unexpected strikes. A key sovereign borrower is downgraded, flashing across global news wires. Within seconds, the tremor is felt in markets: credit spreads widen, liquidity tightens, and counterparties reassess exposures. In a legacy world, Lisa would have convened an emergency call, analysts would scramble through data, and stress scenarios might arrive hours later, too late to lead, just in time to react.

In the agentic institution, the response is immediate. Lisa's volatility agents pivot from passive monitoring to active simulation. In real time, they ingest live market feeds, breaking news sentiment, and CDS movements, layering these inputs against institutional exposures. They do not just watch the market; they test it, running macro-path simulations, stress-testing correlations, and mapping cascading effects on liquidity, funding, and counterparty positions across regions.

Within moments, a narrative briefing surfaces: *"Scenario delta: 45 bps projected impact on liquidity buffers within 12 hours under adverse case. Recommended actions: 1) tighten forward hedges, 2) accelerate regional funding, 3) initiate portfolio review by 5 p.m."* The recommendations are precise, ranked, and contextualized, with confidence levels attached and links to the policies and historical events informing the logic. Lisa does not need to guess what the model meant; the reasoning trail is laid bare.

She does not call a war room. The war room is already in motion. Treasury, risk, and legal teams receive tailored updates from their respective agents, each action plan preloaded and framed against existing guardrails. Governance agents simultaneously check that proposed moves remain within regulatory and institutional boundaries. Stress testing ceases to be a quarterly ritual; it becomes a live reflex, continuously running in the background and surfacing only when action matters.

This orchestration compresses hours of analyst coordination into minutes. Quantitative models, institutional memory, and real-time intelligence converge into a single adaptive response. Lisa remains in control, stepping in where human judgment is irreplaceable. In this case, she overrides one recommendation, choosing a softer trigger point to avoid signaling panic to the market. The system adapts instantly, recalibrating forecasts and action paths without friction. This is not automation for its own sake; it is intelligence designed for collaboration, a co-pilot that knows when to lead and when to yield.

By 4:00 p.m., her teams are aligned, counterparties reassured, and the institution has already repositioned proactively rather than defensively. Volatility, once synonymous with disruption and firefighting, is reframed as a proving ground, a test of institutional reflexes and resilience. In the agentic bank, turbulence does not expose fragility. It reveals capability.

Agent Feedback Loops: Training and Evolution

As her day winds down, Lisa turns to the most strategic part of her routine: agent feedback. Every decision she makes, every override she issues, every insight she flags as valuable is logged, not to police her, but to refine the institution's intelligence. This is not an audit, it is learning in motion.

Each agent in her mesh comes with a training interface where human feedback recalibrates performance in real time. Lisa does not write code or label datasets; she teaches by doing. When she marks a liquidity forecast as "misaligned with intent," the treasury agent updates its reasoning model. When she rewrites a client summary in her own words, the CX agent absorbs not only the structure but also the institutional tone, becoming more aligned with both her expectations and the bank's voice. Over time, these micro-interactions accumulate into something larger: a distributed institutional memory, shaped, refined, and shared across the agentic mesh.

The process is not passive. Her compliance agent proactively surfaces a recommendation: *"Your override pattern indicates higher tolerance for mid-risk counterparties under stable, low-volatility conditions. Suggest adjusting weighting parameters accordingly."* Lisa reviews, tweaks the model, and logs her rationale. The system archives both her decision and her reasoning, creating an explainable, traceable lineage that future regulators, auditors, or colleagues can interrogate. The result is not just a more accurate agent; it is an agentic system that remembers why it was shaped in a particular way.

Crucially, these feedback loops are bounded by governance scaffolds. Not every individual preference becomes institutional policy. Overrides trigger reviews, escalation paths, and safeguards to prevent bias or drift. Feedback is not simply absorbed; it is curated, tested, and reconciled against institutional goals and regulatory constraints. This ensures that what agents learn is not merely the voice of one executive, but the collective intent of the organization.

This is how institutions now evolve. Instead of rewriting policy manuals with every market event, they encode intelligence through interaction. Instead of training agents once and freezing them, they engage in continuous learning loops, where human expertise and machine reasoning converge in real time. Over weeks and months, Lisa is not just supervising agents, she is co-creating them.

In the agentic bank, learning is not a project or a quarterly review. It is embedded in daily work, distributed across systems, and anchored in governance. Humans shape the mesh, and the mesh, in turn, becomes an extension of human intent, an institution that learns, adapts, and evolves in concert with its leaders.

Building Blocks: Implementation Reality

Lisa's world is not science fiction; it is the outcome of deliberate design, layered architecture, and institutional resolve. To build it, banks must reimagine their very foundations. Intelligence must no longer sit at the edges of workflows; it must be woven into the decisioning layer itself. Compliance can no longer be an afterthought applied once transactions are complete; it must operate as part of every interaction. Data can no longer remain locked in silos; it must flow fluidly, continuously, and with full integrity. What emerges is not a technology project, but an operating model transformation that fuses engineering, governance, and culture into a single, adaptive framework.

It begins with the intelligence layer: specialized agents fine-tuned on enterprise data, grounded in retrieval-augmented generation (RAG), and orchestrated across treasury, compliance, client engagement, and beyond. These agents, treasury copilots, compliance sentinels, and client intelligence orchestrators, are not isolated tools but collaborators. They operate in concert, drawing on shared memory stores while remaining bounded by live policy logic that enforces institutional intent.

But intelligence without structure is noise. That is why institutions that deploy agentic systems pair them with a governance mesh: embedded guardrails that monitor agent behavior, enforce escalation paths, and log explainability metadata in real time. This ensures that when agents fail, and they will, they fail gracefully, within known limits, and with a complete audit trail that preserves accountability. Transparency is not bolted on afterward; it is designed into every decision.

A resilient data fabric ties it all together. Historical records, live transaction streams, and external signals, ranging from market feeds to news sentiment, are continuously blended into unified contexts where agents can reason across time horizons. This is what transforms data from static input into a living dialogue, powering decisions that evolve as conditions change.

And yet, even the most elegant architecture will falter without institutional readiness. Lisa's world reflects leaders who chose to redesign workflows instead of digitizing the old ones. It reflects regulators who demand and are granted live oversight, not quarterly reports. It reflects teams who are not displaced but elevated, trained to collaborate with agents, to interrogate reasoning, and to refine institutional intelligence through feedback loops.

This is not a proof-of-concept culture; it is an end-to-end operating model where humans and machines are partners in judgment. Building blocks like intelligence layers, governance meshes, and data fabrics are necessary, but they are not sufficient without leadership clarity, cultural alignment, and regulatory trust. Only when these elements move in concert can institutions shift from incremental digitization to the agentic reality where resilience, adaptability, and trust are embedded by design.

Inside a 12-Month Agentic Pilot

A year before Lisa's institution reached its current state of orchestration, the journey began in treasury. The leadership team resisted the temptation of a sweeping rollout and instead chose a precise entry point: liquidity forecasting. As the CIO recalls:

> *"We didn't start with a big bang. We picked liquidity forecasting as our beachhead, complex enough to prove value but narrow enough to control risk."*

The early months were about foundations. The bank assembled its stack carefully: Azure OpenAI Service as the Large Language Models (LLM) backbone, LangChain as the orchestration framework for retrieval-augmented generation, and Snowflake as the unified data layer. Event streams flowed through Apache Kafka, linking SAP from the ERP side, core banking APIs, and Bloomberg market feeds into what became the institution's first live perception fabric.

Once the foundation was laid, the first treasury agent entered production, cautiously, in advisory-only mode. It monitored intraday liquidity, simulated funding scenarios, and issued recommendations with confidence scores. Every decision was logged in Fiddler.ai for explainability, while escalation and approval rules were enforced by

ServiceNow GRC to ensure that oversight remained firmly human-led.

As confidence grew, governance expanded. Identity and access were secured through Okta, compliance logic was codified in Open Policy Agent, and real-time oversight dashboards streamed continuously into Splunk. What once would have been a bottleneck, compliance review, was reframed as an active enabler of speed, transparency, and trust.

By the end of the first year, orchestration was in motion. Liquidity agents began coordinating with compliance agents to pre-clear major funding moves. Client experience agents surfaced cash flow signals that fed directly into treasury forecasts. The system was no longer siloed; it was a living mesh, where intelligence moved across domains and enriched every decision.

The results spoke for themselves: funding costs reduced by 15 basis points, compliance review time cut by nearly a third, and full audit traceability available to regulators on demand. But beyond the metrics, the cultural shift was even more significant. What began as a controlled experiment had proven that agents could operate safely, transparently, and effectively inside the institution's fabric. It was the quiet but decisive beginning of the agentic transformation that Lisa would later inherit at scale.

The Playbook for Scale

Lisa's world did not materialize overnight. It emerged one use case at a time, each carefully layered into a growing mesh of agents, governance frameworks, and feedback loops. Institutions that succeeded in this transition revealed a familiar rhythm. They started small, often with a single high-value agent in a domain such as anti–money laundering triage, liquidity forecasting, or KYC automation. By proving accuracy, reliability, and trustworthiness in one domain, they earned the credibility to expand further.

This phased approach was supported by a deliberate technology stack. Hyperscaler platforms such as Azure, AWS, or GCP provided the backbone, but were always complemented by fintech-specialized APIs like World-Check or SWIFT gpi, and by observability tools such as WhyLabs for drift detection and Fiddler.ai for explainability. The orchestration was never about a single vendor; it was about weaving together a fabric of capabilities that could evolve with the institution.

Cost and timing discipline became the difference between experiments and enterprise adoption. Institutions typically invested between $2 million and $4 million to run pilots, then scaled with commitments of $8 million to $15 million for full deployment. Timelines stretched over 12 to 18 months, with ROI realized within 18 to 24 months, measured in operational savings, reduced funding costs, and measurable improvements in compliance efficiency.

But even the most disciplined programs faced friction. Legacy cores resisted integration, forcing middleware layers such as MuleSoft to carry the load. Regulatory alignment often slowed progress when explainability standards had not been established upfront, adding review cycles and uncertainty. And cultural resistance proved just as formidable; relationship managers and compliance staff had to learn to trust-but-verify, adjusting to a model where agents were collaborators rather than tools to be second-guessed.

These frictions, however, were not failures. They were reminders that building an agentic institution is as much about alignment as it is about engineering. The institutions that thrived were those that treated every obstacle as a design signal, refining both systems and culture until the organization could operate as one, humans and agents in concert.

From Blueprint to Reality

Lisa's world is not a projection, it is already taking shape. The intelligence layer is no longer theoretical. Large language models fine-tuned on enterprise data and retrieval-augmented generation frameworks are already live in production. Governance meshes are not whiteboard concepts but working systems, with banks deploying real-time audit dashboards accessible to regulators as transactions unfold. The question is no longer *can this be done?* but *how fast can institutions adapt?* In the agentic bank, speed does not come from removing oversight; it comes from building trust into the very architecture, so that compliance and judgment move at the same velocity as decision-making.

Every institution that succeeds in this transition begins with what might be called Day 1 Readiness. The fastest movers are not those with the flashiest models or the biggest AI labs, but those that prepare their data, their governance, and their teams to work in concert from the very beginning.

It starts with the data fabric. Agentic systems depend on unified, high-quality information that flows without friction. Banks that succeed invest early in centralizing structured and unstructured data, and transaction ledgers and client communications alike, on platforms such as Snowflake or Databricks. They connect these to live signals through event streaming backbones like Kafka or Confluent, ensuring treasury flows, payment updates, and trading movements feed continuously into the system. They spend the time to map and cleanse client profiles, risk logs, and compliance histories. Without this, intelligence collapses into noise.

But data alone is not enough. Trust has to be engineered into the system from the outset.

Institutions that embed governance as code, using platforms such as OPA or HashiCorp Sentinel, define guardrails that no agent can cross. They scope agent permissions through identity managers like Okta or Azure AD, ensuring role-specific boundaries. They build real-time audit dashboards with tools such as Splunk, Elastic, or Fiddler.ai, giving compliance teams and regulators live visibility into every reasoning trail. Those who delay this step inevitably face regulatory pushback, because in the agentic era, governance cannot be retrofitted; it must be part of the foundation.

Technology, however, cannot carry this alone. The organizations that thrive form fusion teams that blend business leaders, compliance officers, data scientists, and platform engineers into cross-functional pods. They appoint agent stewards, human overseers tasked with monitoring performance, guiding exceptions, and shaping continuous learning loops. Risk and audit functions are involved from the very beginning, defining explainability requirements before the first pilot goes live. When agents are designed without business and compliance as co-authors, adoption stalls.

Pilots, too, follow a pattern. Institutions move fastest when they start narrow and prove depth before they scale. Liquidity optimization, Anti-Money Laundering (AML) triage, and client experience have emerged as natural starting points: use cases that are complex enough to show value but contained enough to manage risk. Deployed over six to nine months, these pilots succeed when they are measured against hard metrics, decision accuracy, override rates, and efficiency gains, rather than vague innovation promises.

And underneath it all lies culture. Agents are not tools to be switched on; they are digital colleagues to be guided, corrected, and trusted. Institutions that normalize feedback loops, where overrides and escalations are reviewed weekly to refine reasoning, build confidence. Relationship managers who start their day with agent briefings or compliance teams that run weekly decision clinics learn to see agents as amplifiers rather than threats. Where culture is ignored, adoption falters. Where culture is designed, collaboration flourishes.

This is how Lisa's world comes into being, not through sudden transformation, but through the discipline of building the right foundations on day one.

The First Step

These are not futuristic prerequisites; they are actions institutions can begin today. Preparing data, embedding governance, and forming fusion teams is not a delay of innovation; it is the essence of responsible innovation. The banks that invest six months in these foundations are not falling behind. They are ensuring that when intelligence arrives, it does so safely, explainably, and at scale.

Lisa's institution followed that path. It resisted the temptation to rush into proofs of concept and instead built the scaffolding first. Only then did it launch its first liquidity agent, not as an experiment but as a controlled, auditable deployment that regulators, risk officers, and leadership could trust from day one. That initial trust was the lever. It turned a single use case into a platform for expansion, into cross-functional orchestration, live compliance integration, and, eventually, a world where agents and humans operate side by side with confidence.

The lesson is simple but decisive: the future does not begin with a leap; it begins with a first step. And that first step determines whether agentic systems remain pilots at the edges or become the very fabric of the institution.

What follows in this book is a closer look at how that fabric is woven. If Lisa's world illustrates the destination, the chapters ahead explore the architecture, governance, and leadership that make it possible. We will move from vision to design, from lived examples to the technical and organizational blueprints that bring them to life. In short, we leave the *what* of the agentic institution to begin exploring the *how*.

Chapter 3

ARCHITECTING AGENTIC SYSTEMS

I n the fast-changing world of modern finance, intelligence alone doesn't get the job done. What truly matters is the ability to apply that intelligence in ways that fit the situation and deliver meaningful outcomes.

Many AI initiatives fall short because they focus on producing insights without creating a path for those insights to drive action. A system that generates useful information still depends on people to interpret and apply it, a dependency that can slow progress, introduce risk, or result in missed opportunities.

Agentic systems are designed to close that gap. They are built not only to understand what's happening but also to decide what should happen next. Within carefully defined boundaries, they can take initiative and adapt as conditions change.

To make this possible, institutions must decide where independent action makes sense and where human oversight should step in. Leaders should ask:

- Under what conditions should agents act independently?
- Where should escalation or human validation occur?
- What types of memory, reasoning, and feedback loops should govern these agents?

These decisions define how the system operates and the level of trust it earns from those who rely on it.

When intelligence is put to work deliberately, accountably, and responsively, it becomes part of how the organization moves forward, not just a tool it uses.

Understanding Agentic Systems

Agents vs. Automation vs. AI

Knowing this redefinition of intelligence, we must distinguish between agentic systems, automation, and generative AI. They may overlap in tools and outputs, but they differ fundamentally in purpose, behavior, and design philosophy.

Automation is rule-based. It performs repeatable tasks according to predefined logic. Think robotic process automation (RPA), batch scheduling, or triggered workflows. While automation increases speed and consistency, it has no awareness, adaptability, or goal orientation. It's efficient, but static.

AI, in the enterprise context, refers to data-driven systems that analyze, predict, or classify. These models support decisions, uncover insights, and generate content, but they don't act independently. AI extends cognition, but still depends on a human or system to interpret and act on its output.

In short:
- Automation follows rules.
- AI informs decisions.
- Agents pursue outcomes.

Consider a compliance scenario:
- An automation script might flag a transaction and route it for review.

- An AI model might assign a risk score based on patterns.
- An agent, however, does both and then decides whether to block, escalate, request more data, or auto-resolve, depending on dynamic rules, user history, and environmental context.

This layered capability—perceive, reason, act—is what makes agentic systems transformative. But it also means they must be governed like collaborators, not tools.

The Core Capabilities of an Agent

To build agentic systems that are scalable, safe, and strategically aligned, institutions must begin with a clear understanding of what makes an agent *an agent*.

At a minimum, every agent must possess five foundational attributes:

- Perception, the ability to continuously observe system state, data streams, and contextual signals. This is a dynamic sense of what's happening from macro conditions to user intent to infrastructure status. Since incomplete perception leads to bad decisions, ask: What data should the agent have access to? How often should it update? Who defines the scope of its visibility?

- Reasoning, the ability to interpret context and determine the most appropriate course of action. This includes goal alignment, constraint handling, trade-off evaluation, and policy navigation. Reasoning is what turns data into a decision with an explanation of how. This means building in explainability and justifiability as first-class features, not afterthoughts.
- Action, the ability to initiate, modify, or halt operations within a bounded domain. Whether triggering a payment, adjusting a threshold, or escalating an anomaly, this capacity separates agents from tools: they don't just recommend; they *do*, with the human gating the permissions, contextual thresholds, and oversight mechanisms.
- Alignment, the ability to operate in accordance with institutional values, goals, and risk tolerances. Alignment must be encoded, not assumed, connecting agent autonomy and enterprise control. It is a continuously updated representation of what the institution *wants* to happen under different conditions. This includes risk appetite, strategic objectives, and reputational boundaries.
- Learning, the ability to adapt behavior based on feedback, new data, and changes in the environment. Agents must track outcomes, adapt heuristics, and avoid repeating errors.

But learning must be bounded. To ensure an agent doesn't cut corners, you teach it how to serve goals more effectively within acceptable limits. Without learning, agents become brittle. With it, they evolve with the institution.

You can't treat any of these as optional. Miss one, and the system reverts to something less powerful and far less trustworthy.

Once these capabilities are established, the next step is defining how agents operate within the enterprise. Not all agents will look the same, nor should they. A treasury agent coordinating liquidity decisions has a different scope, latency, and risk boundaries than a client-facing agent managing personalized recommendations.

Different types of agents need different approaches. A compliance agent has to be much more careful about following rules than a marketing agent that's trying to personalize recommendations. A well-designed agent in compliance will emphasize constraint adherence and traceability. A marketing agent may prioritize adaptation and behavioral modeling. Same capabilities, different expressions.

Agent Roles, Boundaries, and Goals

Designing agent roles is as important as building the agents themselves.

Each agent role should be defined by three key dimensions:

- Purpose: What is the agent trying to achieve? This is the outcome it's optimized for, whether it's maximizing liquidity efficiency, ensuring regulatory compliance, or personalizing client engagement. Purpose anchors behavior.
- Scope: What domain does the agent operate within? Scope includes both data access (e.g., systems, feeds, and client segments) and action authority (e.g., can it initiate transactions or only suggest?). Narrow scope improves control; broad scope increases leverage, and both must be intentional.
- Boundaries: What limits must the agent respect? These include risk thresholds, escalation triggers, business logic, ethical constraints, and regulatory rules.

Defining these elements clearly ensures that agents do not drift from their mission, exceed their authority, or introduce unintended consequences, but note that these are not static definitions. As institutions evolve, so must the roles. And as agents learn, their boundaries may expand or contract, depending on trust levels, outcome quality, and regulatory changes.

Such agent-to-agent coordination must be intentionally designed and governed.

And just like with human roles, these parameters must be reviewed, audited, and refined over time. Institutions must also consider role hierarchies. Not all agents are peers. Some agents supervise or coordinate others. Some operate autonomously; others support human collaborators.

Once agent roles are defined, the challenge becomes operational: How do we enforce boundaries without stifling intelligence? How do we ensure agents remain aligned as goals evolve, data shifts, or edge cases arise?

The answer lies in three layers of constraint:

- Architectural constraints are hard-coded into the systems, access control, API permissions, and data segregation. These ensure agents operate only within authorized zones. For example, a lending agent may access underwriting models and credit data, but not client transaction history unless explicitly allowed. These are your first line of defense. Beyond these constraints, agents must possess self-awareness to recognize uncertainty and appropriately escalate decisions.

- Behavioral constraints are embedded into the agent's logic, encoded rules, decision frameworks, and institutional heuristics. These guide how the agent interprets situations and what actions it's allowed to consider. Think of them as internalized policy. A treasury agent might rebalance positions within tolerance bands but must escalate if deviation exceeds thresholds or timing risk emerges.

- Supervisory constraints are dynamic, based on monitoring, feedback loops, and human-in-the-loop oversight. These allow institutions to intervene when agents encounter ambiguous data, conflicting goals, or novel scenarios. For instance, a client experience agent may operate autonomously but pause for approval when sentiment signals are inconsistent with client profile.

Most importantly, agents need to know when they're in over their heads. If an agent isn't sure about something, it should ask for help instead of guessing.

With this foundation, every agent must act with purpose, but in complex institutions, that purpose must be contextualized. An agent's local objective (e.g., optimizing cash flow) must align with global priorities (e.g., liquidity risk, regulatory exposure, reputational guardrails). Misalignment leads to silent failures: technically sound decisions that damage enterprise value.

This is why goal encoding is essential. Agents need to go beyond tasks and into principles understanding not just *what* to do, but *why* it matters, and *when* to adapt.

There are three levels at which goals must be defined:

- Functional Goals, Task-specific outcomes: rebalance accounts, route service requests, monitor Know Your Customer (KYC) updates. These are concrete, measurable, and easy to benchmark.
- Institutional Goals, Broader objectives: maximize client satisfaction, minimize operational risk, ensure policy compliance. These often involve trade-offs and prioritization.
- Ethical and Strategic Goals, Values that govern decision-making when logic alone is insufficient. For example, respecting client dignity in automated interactions or deferring action in high-risk ambiguity. These principles are encoded in institutional DNA.

Agents constantly face trade-offs. Should they prioritize speed or accuracy? Efficiency or compliance? So they need clear guidance on how to handle these conflicts and when to ask a human for help. That's why agent design cannot be siloed. Business, risk, tech, and compliance must co-author goals and constraints. When agents reflect this shared intent, they become more than tools. They become trusted collaborators.

Architecting the Agentic Stack

When Ravi Patel logged into his treasury console in Singapore, the overnight picture was already clear. His liquidity agent had rebalanced idle cash across currencies, flagged a funding gap two weeks out, and paused a high-value transfer for review.

It wasn't the pause that caught his attention, it was what happened next. His risk agent, overseen by Amira Khan, validated the FX exposure, confirmed limits were safe, and cleared the transfer. Moments later, Diego Morales, head of compliance, sent a short message: "Reviewed and approved, auto-audit logged."

Ravi didn't touch a thing. The agents, and the architecture behind them, had done the work.

This is what happens when a bank runs on what we call the agentic stack: a modular system designed for agents that don't just automate; they observe, reason, act, and learn as part of the institution itself.

The six layers of agency in action

The stack operates like a living system, each layer reinforcing the next:
- Perception Layer: The sensory grid. Ravi's liquidity agent continuously pulls ERP balances, FX feeds, and risk signals. Without it, agents operate blind, no better than humans staring at yesterday's data.

- Memory Layer: Institutional recall. When yen volatility disrupted transfers last quarter, that exception, and Amira's override, was logged. This time, the agent recognized the pattern and pre-emptively paused.
- Reasoning Layer: The brain. The agent didn't just see volatility; it understood it exceeded limits and escalated before acting.
- Action Layer: Execution pathways. Routine USD-to-EUR sweeps are completed automatically, but GBP transfers above $10M paused pending review.
- Governance Layer: Trust enforcers. Identity permissions capped Ravi's liquidity agent's authority, while every move was recorded for Diego's audit team.
- Orchestration Layer: The conductor. This is where the Risk and Liquidity Agents "spoke," validated exposure, synchronized actions, and resumed execution, all logged, transparent, and traceable.

Each layer on its own is valuable. Together, they turn autonomous agents into institutional actors you can trust.

Operationalizing Agent Roles

Ravi's liquidity agent wasn't improvising. Its role was deliberately defined:

- Purpose: Maintain liquidity buffers while minimizing idle capital.
- Scope: Access ERP balances, FX feeds, and internal banking APIs. Execute internal sweeps autonomously but escalate interbank transfers above $10M.
- Boundaries: Halt and escalate if FX volatility exceeds 3%, liquidity buffers drop below 105%, or if forecast models conflict.

These parameters didn't just protect the bank, they let Ravi delegate confidently, knowing exactly when the agent would stop and ask for help.

A well-designed agent acts like a trusted deputy. A poorly defined one behaves like an intern with a master key.

Well-Defined Agent	Poorly Defined Agent
Specific goal: Optimize liquidity	Vague: "Manage cash"
Scoped API access: ERP & FX only	Broad access: All banking systems
Boundaries: Escalates at $10M	No triggers: Errors caught after

Ravi's agent earned trust because its purpose, scope, and boundaries were explicit, reviewed quarterly, and embedded in governance.

When volatility hit, the liquidity agent paused and queried Amira's risk agent. Within seconds, the agents exchanged exposure data, aligned priorities, and resumed action. This "ask, confirm, execute" protocol wasn't ad hoc; it was built into the orchestration layer, ensuring agents coordinate like colleagues, not competing bots.

Operating and Scaling Agentic Systems

Making Autonomy Safe

Before launch, his liquidity agent went through:
- Stress testing: Simulated against crises from 2008 to COVID.
- Staged rollout: Started in read-only mode, then limited execution under review.
- Governance sign-off: Treasury, risk, and compliance all approved.
- Version control: Policy updates tracked and reversible within minutes.

Diego summed it up in one leadership meeting: "Autonomy isn't risk. Unsupervised autonomy is risk."

Avoiding Common Pitfalls

Even with this rigor, Ravi has seen what happens when discipline slips:
- Over-permissioned agents drift beyond their lane.

- Role definitions are left untouched as policies change.
- No rollback occurs when an update misfires.

Their fix? Least-privilege access. Quarterly role reviews. Mandatory rollback paths. In this model, autonomy doesn't mean loss of control; it means building control in advance.

Scaling Beyond Treasury

Treasury was the proving ground. From there, the same stack extended horizontally:
- Risk agents tied market data directly to funding decisions.
- Compliance agents automated regulatory checks and audit trails.
- Client engagement agents delivered proactive portfolio alerts for relationship managers.

Each new agent plugged into the same layers: perception, reasoning, governance, orchestration, and compounding institutional intelligence.

The Leadership View

In quarterly reviews, Ravi and his peers no longer ask, *"How many transactions did we process?"* They ask:

- Are agents staying within boundaries?
- Are escalations the exception or the norm?
- Is orchestration resolving conflicts or surfacing them faster?

These are not IT questions. They are design diagnostics for an institution that now thinks and acts in real time.

We'll explore the cultural and organizational implications of this in chapter 5.

Architecture as Advantage

Ravi's team doesn't just process faster; they decide faster, with confidence. FX exposure isn't caught at quarter-end, it's flagged in motion. Compliance isn't a checklist, it's continuous.

This is the promise of the agentic stack: distributed agency, coordinated action, and trust encoded in design.

In this world, architecture is a competitive strategy, written in code.

Designing for Trust

The central premise is simple: Designing for trust is designing for adoption. If stakeholders, clients, regulators, employees, and partners don't understand how decisions are made or how outcomes are governed, they will resist. And resistance kills performance.

Trust in agentic systems depends on three factors:

- Transparency: Can users and stakeholders understand what the agent did and why?
- Alignment: Are the agent's goals, constraints, and values consistent with institutional intent?
- Accountability: Who is responsible when agents err, and how can the system adapt?

These dimensions are not abstract ideals; they're operational design principles. The table below frames each trust factor as a practical question and ties it to specific system behaviors:

Trust Factor	Institutional Question	System Behavior Needed
Transparency	Do I understand what the agent did and why?	Narrated reasoning, inspectable decisions
Alignment	Is the agent pursuing the right goals with the right rules?	Policy-scoped action, value-matched outputs
Accountability	Who owns outcomes, and how do we learn from failures?	Escalation maps, retraining loops, override records

These elements must be embedded in the system's architecture, not treated as afterthoughts or ethical add-ons.

Institutions that prioritize these factors will unlock scale, speed, and satisfaction. Those that don't will find their systems sidelined, not for lack of capability but for lack of credibility.

The rise of agentic systems marks a shift in where trust is earned and lost. In traditional systems, trust is grounded in processes: checklists, sign-offs, and review cycles. In agentic systems, trust depends on logic: reasoning models, boundary constraints, and feedback loops. The medium has changed and so must the design principles.

Functional versus strategic trust

It's crucial to distinguish between functional and strategic trust.

Functional trust is built when agents perform tasks reliably, explain decisions clearly, and escalate appropriately, delivering operational confidence.

Strategic trust emerges when stakeholders believe that the system's goals align with theirs and that it can adapt as conditions evolve.

Functional trust stems from technical excellence, strategic trust from institutional clarity. This clarity must be encoded in goals, roles, and response protocols. Without clear alignment, even accurate decisions can feel arbitrary, confusing clients and frustrating staff.

For example, consider an agent that declines a loan. If the rationale is opaque or contradicts a previously approved case, trust erodes. However, if the decision is explainable, consistent with policy, and offers recourse, trust is reinforced because the process was credible.

Explainability and alignment

In finance, trust depends on clarity. If stakeholders cannot understand what an agent did and why, every decision risks becoming a black box, and black boxes are unacceptable.

Explainability is a design discipline. Agents must be built to narrate their reasoning in real time and in plain language. Every output should be paired with a transparent reasoning trail that stakeholders can interrogate, trace, and, if necessary, override.

Static dashboards visualize data. They present charts and numbers but leave interpretation, and accountability, to human operators. But now interfaces must evolve into explainability consoles: narrative-driven, interactive environments that expose how and why each decision was made.

These consoles allow users to:
- View outcomes alongside confidence levels and applied policies.
- Trace step-by-step reasoning chains.
- Inspect supporting evidence at the source.
- Override or escalate decisions with full audit logging.

An effective console includes:

- Decision Summary
  - » Outcome with confidence score (e.g., "Loan Application: Declined").
  - » Agent signature, version number, timestamp, and applied policy (e.g., "Risk Model v3.4, Lending Policy Rev. 2025-Q1").

- Reasoning Path (expandable steps showing causal logic with each step linked directly to its data source)
  - » Cash Flow Volatility: Exceeded policy threshold (6.2% vs. 5%).
  - » Collateral Value: Fell 12% below benchmark.
  - » Engagement Score: Low repayment confidence (58/100).

- Evidence Panel
  - » Supporting documents (e.g., statements, appraisals, ERP extracts), timestamped and source-traced.

- Override and Feedback
  - » Structured override workflow requiring justification, feeding agent retraining loops.

- Audit and Version Control
  - » Immutable logs with "version diffs" showing how reasoning evolved between model iterations.

This layered approach shifts explainability from static reporting to live, inspectable reasoning.

To make explainability tangible and implementable, the following table outlines the core components of an agentic console and their respective functions:

Component	Function	Examples / Details
Decision Summary	Presents the outcome, confidence, and governing logic	- Outcome: *Loan Application Declined* - Confidence: *92%* - Agent: *Risk Model v3.4*
Reasoning Path	Shows step-by-step causal chain, each tied to a specific signal	- Step 1: *Cash Flow Volatility* exceeded threshold - Step 2: *Collateral Value* dropped 12%
Evidence Panel	Links to underlying data sources used in reasoning	- Source docs: *Bank statements, market valuations, ERP pulls* - Each entry timestamped and labeled
Override Interface	Allows human escalation with structured justification and agent retraining input	- Action: *Override approved by credit officer* - Justification: *Temporary liquidity spike*
Audit Log & Version Control	Immutable record of decisions, overrides, model version history, and policy alignment	- Diff: *Risk Model updated from v3.3 to v3.4* - Logged: *Aug 22, 2025, 14:03 UTC*

Together, these layers form a structured interface for institutional trust, turning agent outputs into transparent, inspectable reasoning that supports oversight, auditability, and human confidence.

Chapter 4

USE CASES IN ACTION

As agentic banking is being applied across core functions of the modern financial institution, from treasury and client experience to compliance and ESG, we have real use cases demonstrating the transformative potential of goal-directed, feedback-enabled agents that operate across traditional boundaries.

Each use case in this chapter answers a few critical questions:

- What problem is the agent solving, and why now?
- How does the agent interact with systems, data, and people?
- What changes in the institutional operating model?
- What business impact has been observed or projected?

The Overnight Fix: Agentic Treasury in Action

Treasury management is where banks handle their most critical daily decisions about cash, risk, and timing. It's also where AI agents can have the biggest immediate impact. Liquidity management, funding strategies, intraday forecasting, and currency optimization are domains that demand precision, speed, and adaptability. Yet most treasury systems still rely on batched data, rigid workflows, and manual escalations. In a world of 24/7 markets and instant settlement expectations, this model is no longer sustainable. Plus, it is dangerous.

Agentic systems change the calculus. To illustrate this, consider this scenario:

At 4:13 a.m. in Singapore, Maya should have been asleep. But across the bank's global treasury network, billions were moving. An unusually large intercompany transfer had triggered a liquidity imbalance in Frankfurt. Maya didn't get an alert, though. She didn't need to. The agent did its job.

Here's what happened: The treasury agent continuously monitors cash flows against predetermined thresholds. When Frankfurt's position dropped below the minimum buffer of €50 million, the agent immediately accessed real-time balances across all regional entities. It identified €75 million in available funds in Zurich, calculated the optimal transfer amount to restore both locations to target levels, and executed the rebalancing within regulatory parameters, all in under 30 seconds.

No overdraft. No panic. By the time Maya reviewed the audit trail over coffee, she was already free to plan funding scenarios for a coming rate hike.

This represents a fundamental shift in how treasury operates. Traditional systems would have generated an alert, waited for human review, required manual approval, and executed the transfer hours later. The agent compressed this timeline from hours to seconds while maintaining full auditability and compliance.

Building the system

Translating this transformation into practice requires careful system design. Implementing an agentic treasury doesn't start with AI; it starts with clarity of intent. What outcomes should the system optimize for? What constraints must it respect? What escalation paths ensure trust and accountability?

These questions form the design brief for agentic architecture. Unlike traditional automation, which is often retrofitted onto existing workflows, agentic treasury systems require composability from the start. The architecture must allow agents to observe across silos, act across systems, and learn across cycles.

Real-world results

At a leading global institution, the implementation of agentic treasury began with a focused objective: reduce intraday liquidity risk across regional entities while minimizing idle balances.

The institution deployed a suite of agents across its TMS and liquidity platforms. These agents were granted narrow, observable scopes, limited to monitoring specific accounts, forecasting short-term positions, and executing predefined rebalancing strategies. For example, one agent focused exclusively on USD flows, tracking high-volume settlement accounts and triggering reallocations based on end-of-day thresholds and inbound clearing activity. Another monitored short-term balances in local currencies across regional hubs, initiating FX swaps or internal transfers when projected deviations exceeded tolerance bands. By distributing cognitive load across specialized agents, the institution established a continuously adaptive liquidity layer, intelligent, precise, and governed.

Across key corridors, institutions saw a meaningful reduction in idle balances as agentic systems introduced real-time visibility and proactive liquidity orchestration. By continuously monitoring flows, forecasting needs, and initiating timely actions, these intelligent agents helped treasury teams unlock trapped value and align liquidity with operational intent, turning static reserves into strategic assets.

Manual interventions for shortfalls declined significantly, as intelligent agents continuously monitored positions, forecasted demand, and initiated rebalancing actions before issues surfaced. What once required reactive attention now unfolded through anticipatory logic, freeing treasury teams to focus on strategy rather than fire drills. In this shift, static reserves transformed into strategic assets, and operational resilience became an embedded capability, not a manual workaround.

More importantly, confidence in agent autonomy increased. Because actions were explainable, consistent, and bounded, treasury professionals began to trust agents as teammates, not just tools.

This success catalyzed expansion into adjacent domains: FX exposure management, regulatory buffer optimization, and inter-entity lending. Each deployment is built on the same architecture, shared perception, distributed reasoning, and orchestrated action.

The lesson was clear: Agentic systems scale not by volume but by alignment. When agents understand their purpose, operate within trustworthy constraints, and evolve through feedback, they unlock exponential efficiency without exponential complexity.

Treasury, once a reactive function, became an active orchestrator through a fundamental shift in design philosophy.

Client Experience and Personalization

While treasury operations showcase agentic systems' impact on internal processes, client experience demonstrates their external value. Client experience has always been a strategic differentiator, but in the era of digital saturation, personalization is an expectation. Clients expect one outcome, not ten dashboards. They want to be understood rather than merely guided.

Agentic systems are making that possible, not through more interfaces, but through intelligent orchestration behind the scenes. The future of client experience is agent-led CX that operates with a clear purpose behind the scenes.

They monitor behavior, interpret intent, and proactively deliver value across channels. Whether suggesting a tailored credit product, detecting client friction in real time, or auto-adjusting communication cadence based on preferences, these agents serve as relationship stewards.

Elena stared at her laptop screen, the glow harsh in her darkened home office. 10:47 p.m., and she was still waiting for two clients to pay their invoices. The design firm's checking account showed $3,200, enough to cover payroll, but not the office rent due Friday.

She opened her banking app and scrolled through her options. A business line of credit caught her eye, but the application looked complicated. Twenty questions about revenue projections and collateral. She'd have to dig up tax returns, bank statements, and profit and loss reports. Not tonight.

Elena closed the app and rubbed her eyes. She'd call the business banker tomorrow.

But when she reopened the app to check her balance one more time, something had changed. A new notification appeared: "Elena, we noticed you've been researching credit options. Based on your account history and cash flow patterns, you're pre-approved for a $25,000 working capital line. No paperwork needed. Funds available immediately."

The terms were perfect, a revolving line that matched her typical invoice cycle. Elena tapped "Accept" and watched her available balance jump to $28,200. Crisis averted.

Behind the scenes, her bank's agent had been watching. It noticed her late-night login, the time spent on the credit pages, and the pattern of invoice delays that happened every few months. The agent recognized financial stress and responded with exactly what Elena needed, when she needed it.

By Thursday, Elena had received a text asking if she needed help setting up the line of credit. By Friday, another agent had sent tips for faster invoice collection. It felt like the bank was actually paying attention to her business.

"It's like they read my mind," she told her business partner. For the first time in months, Elena felt like she had a financial partner, not just a bank account.

Agentic advantage

Elena's experience illustrates the agentic advantage. The shift is profound:

- Traditional personalization was static, based on segments and rule-based logic.
- Modern personalization is dynamic, adapting in real time to micro-behaviors and contextual signals.
- AI agents can figure out what customers actually want, not just what category they fit into. The key difference is that these AI systems learn to predict what customers need before customers even ask, which is helpful in this "Do It For Me" era, where value is measured not in features but in friction removed.

This approach delivers two main benefits: happier customers and lower costs.

Designing for trust

While this practice intelligence creates opportunity, designing for trust requires addressing important questions:
When should agents act autonomously vs. recommend? Elena's credit approval was automated because the risk was low and the need was immediate. But larger credit decisions or investment recommendations might require human partnership.

How do we encode tone, empathy, and appropriateness into agent behavior? Agents must understand not just what clients need, but how they prefer to receive it. Some clients want immediate action; others prefer to review options first.

What escalation paths exist when personalization fails or causes confusion? Agents must recognize when their interventions aren't welcome and gracefully defer to human colleagues.

To address these, institutions must define CX governance models. Agents must be trained not just on data, but on values. For example, never upsell when a client shows distress signals. Always offer opt-outs. Ensure transparency on how decisions are made.

Agentic CX helps earn client confidence at scale.

Real-world results

At a major regional bank focused on SME clients, the introduction of agentic CX began with a deceptively simple use case: onboarding follow-through. Too many clients dropped off during onboarding, not due to friction in process, but due to distraction, uncertainty, or lack of support.

Instead of sending reminder emails or queuing service calls, the bank deployed a cohort of onboarding agents. These agents had three core tasks:
- Detect abandonment or delay points.
- Infer potential causes based on behavior patterns.
- Deliver personalized nudges or human interventions based on client context.

Within just a few months of deploying agent-assisted onboarding, the bank observed a clear lift in completion rates and a noticeable reduction in client drop-off. The experience became smoother, more responsive, and tailored to the individual's journey, resulting in faster progression from initial engagement to active participation. Clients supported by intelligent agents throughout onboarding were also more likely to continue into deeper, value-generating relationships, reinforcing the strategic advantage of embedding agency into the earliest stages of the client lifecycle.

But the larger impact was cultural. Product teams began thinking in agentic terms: What parts of the client journey are currently passive? Where could agents reduce friction or enhance engagement without introducing complexity?

Soon the agents were expanded to manage credit product discovery, digital self-service support, and churn prediction for high-value clients. Each new deployment followed the same principle: predict, personalize, and partner.

The takeaway was clear: The real value isn't just saving money or moving faster. It's building customer trust and learning what actually works.

Dynamic Risk Monitoring in an Agentic Bank

Dynamic monitoring agents operate continuously across institutional boundaries, ingesting live signals, detecting anomalies, and escalating threats in real time.

These agents run as an always-on institutional nervous system, scanning the bank's core infrastructure, external intelligence, and market environment without pause.

How monitoring agents connect

Dynamic monitoring agents interface directly with the institution's operational backbone:

- Core Banking Systems (CBS): Accessing transaction ledgers and account histories to identify unusual flows.
- Payment Networks & Clearing Systems: Tracking SWIFT, Fedwire, SEPA, and instant payment rails in motion.

- Enterprise Risk & Compliance Tools: Linking to Anti-Money Laundering (AML) platforms, sanctions screening engines, and fraud detection tools.
- Market & Trading Platforms: Drawing from real-time pricing feeds, exposure books, and risk analytics.
- External Intelligence Feeds: Consuming sanctions lists, adverse media, and regulatory bulletins contextualized through retrieval-augmented generation (RAG).

The data they use

Dynamic risk monitoring relies on a layered data fabric:
- Transactional Data: Cash movements, cross-border transfers, and high-risk transaction types.
- Behavioral Profiles: Baselines built from historical patterns and peer-group comparisons.
- External Alerts & Feeds: Cyber-threat reports, regulatory watchlists, and sentiment signals from media.
- Internal Risk Logs: Audit records, prior escalations, and resolved cases for pattern recognition.

This combination creates a live, evolving view of institutional risk.

How agents define "deviation"

Deviation is context-driven. Agents don't just apply static rules, they use probabilistic reasoning informed by client context and institutional memory:
- Transaction Anomalies: Spikes in value, frequency, or geography inconsistent with history.
- Behavioral Inconsistencies: Activities outside expected baselines or peer benchmarks.
- Pattern Similarities: Matches to fraud typologies, sanctions evasion methods, or historical case memory.

By distinguishing true risks from benign outliers, agents reduce false positives while accelerating genuine threat detection.

Thresholds and escalation

Risk thresholds are tiered, adaptive, and regulatory-aligned.
Tiered:
- Level 1: Advisory alerts surfaced to analysts.
- Level 2: Low-risk dismissals handled autonomously (e.g., recurring benign patterns).
- Level 3: High-confidence cases escalated per compliance playbooks.

Adaptive: Continuously recalibrated using analyst feedback and historical outcomes.

Regulatory-Aligned: Mapped directly to AML, fraud, and supervisory standards.

This approach embeds compliance rigor into every detection layer.

Implementation in practice

Deploying dynamic monitoring agents follows a measured, governance-by-design approach:

1. Overlay agents onto existing AML and fraud systems in observation mode.
2. Connect via APIs to payment, market, and compliance systems for richer context.
3. Run supervised loops where agents propose actions, analysts validate, and feedback refines precision.
4. Expand autonomy gradually, moving from advisory to bounded execution as accuracy improves and trust builds.

The result is not a bolt-on compliance tool, but a live institutional capability, risk detection that is continuous, adaptive, and deeply embedded in the bank's fabric.

Agentic AML in Action

Marcus Alvarez, Head of Financial Crime Compliance at a global bank, was facing a familiar challenge: his analysts were overwhelmed by false-positive AML alerts. Most of their time was spent clearing benign cases, leaving little room for deep investigation into truly suspicious activity.

"It felt like we were firefighting every day," Marcus admitted. "We had alerts coming from everywhere, but no way to separate noise from genuine risk efficiently."

To tackle this, Marcus's institution introduced agentic AML triage agents. These weren't new detection systems but reasoning agents layered on top of their existing rule-based tools, built to prioritize what mattered most.

How Marcus's AML agents worked

Each agent connected securely to:
- Client histories to establish behavioral baselines.
- External watchlists such as sanctions lists and politically exposed persons (PEPs).
- Historical analyst decisions from prior investigations.
- Behavioral patterns drawn from peer benchmarks and institutional data.

With this intelligence, the agents began triaging alerts dynamically:
- Auto-dismissing repetitive false positives that matched prior cleared cases.
- Auto-escalating high-confidence threats linked to known risk typologies.
- Routing ambiguous alerts directly to human analysts for deeper investigation.

The impact in practice

Within weeks, the effect was evident:
- The burden of false positives fell sharply, freeing analysts to focus on high-complexity cases.
- Alert resolution became faster, reducing backlog and response times.
- Internal audit teams gained confidence thanks to transparent decision logs and explainability.

Critically, the agents didn't run unchecked. They learned continuously from analyst feedback, refining their reasoning within clear, auditable rules. Human oversight stayed firmly in place, but repetitive triage work shifted to agents.

Scaling Safely with Tiered Governance

To expand this success across risk and compliance functions, Marcus's team applied tiered governance:

- Level 1 – Advisory: Agents act as advisors, flagging risks and recommending actions while humans retain full control.
- Level 2 – Controlled Execution: Agents handle low-risk dismissals under strict thresholds but escalate anything uncertain.
- Level 3 – Autonomous Playbooks: Agents operate within defined compliance playbooks, prioritizing cases, escalating based on learned patterns, and reporting outcomes, while humans review exceptions and oversee policy updates.

Across every level, explainability, auditability, and regulatory alignment are core. All actions remain traceable and contestable, ensuring compliance is real-time, adaptive, and transparent.

ESG and Intelligent Reporting

ESG reporting has shifted from a compliance afterthought to a strategic differentiator. Yet for most institutions, it remains fragmented, manual, and reactive. Data silos, inconsistent methodologies, and lengthy assurance cycles erode both credibility and cost efficiency.

Agentic systems change this equation.

The ESG agentic model

ESG agents operate as intelligent collaborators across the reporting lifecycle:

- Data Ingestion: Pulling metrics from internal systems, IoT sensors, and external providers across environmental, labor, governance, and community dimensions.
- Validation: Reconciling inputs to recognized standards (GRI, TCFD, ISSB) and tailoring outputs to evolving investor and regulator demands.
- Anomaly Detection: Flagging discrepancies, delays, or mismatches for immediate review.
- Narrative Assembly: Drafting disclosures and dashboards that link metrics to materiality and stakeholder priorities.

These agents not only enforce compliance, they benchmark performance, surface trends, and optimize narratives, shifting ESG from cost burden to trust accelerator.

Real-world transformation: Aisha's ESG overhaul

Aisha Mensah, Chief Sustainability Officer at a multinational firm operating in over 40 markets, was stuck in the ESG reporting grind. Environmental data sat with operations, social impact metrics with HR, governance measures with legal, each in incompatible formats. Every reporting cycle meant weeks of manual reconciliation, delayed reviews, and competing narratives.

To change this, Aisha's team deployed a coordinated suite of ESG agents:
- Environmental Agent: Monitoring energy consumption, emissions, and waste outputs across facilities.
- Governance & Social Agent: Tracking labor policies, board diversity, whistleblower reports, and policy adherence.
- Contextual Agent: Mapping all data to shifting regulatory standards and investor benchmarks, while aligning outputs to the firm's stated ESG priorities.

Within a short period:
- Manual reconciliations were dramatically reduced.
- Materiality scoring became dynamic, updating as external expectations shifted.
- Internal ESG ratings converged with investor assessments, boosting credibility.

- Reporting lag dropped from lengthy cycles to near real-time responsiveness.

The institution even began answering investor and regulator inquiries on demand, moving from reactive disclosure to proactive leadership.

Aisha reflected, "This was continuous assurance. ESG became something we could *prove*, in real time."

This transformation underscored a larger truth: ESG is not only about what you track, but how quickly and transparently you can prove it.

In agentic systems, credibility is composable. Transparency is scalable. ESG stops being a static report and becomes a living capability, woven directly into the institution's operations.

Orchestrated Intelligence: The Next Leap

As ESG agents integrate with treasury, compliance, client experience, and risk, orchestration becomes the next frontier. Unlike legacy systems built on brittle, hard-coded workflows, agentic systems coordinate dynamically: decentralized reasoning, adaptive negotiation, and shared context.

Orchestration enables:
- Cross-Domain Response: Treasury agents adjust liquidity strategies in response to ESG-driven operational changes.

- Mutual Feedback: Compliance agents re-fine risk thresholds using market volatility flagged by ESG agents.
- Unified Action: All agents resolve conflicts based on institutional goals and real-time priorities.

To achieve this, organizations must build:
- Inter-Agent Protocols: Securing data sharing, state synchronization, and conflict resolution.
- Policy Engines: Codifying cross-functional goals and trade-off rules.
- Human Oversight Layers: Retaining strategic judgment, with clear escalation paths.

When done right, orchestration turns a network of specialized agents into an adaptive, cohesive institution. This is where agentic banking crosses from capability to competitive advantage: where intelligence doesn't sit in dashboards, it is expressed through the institution itself.

Chapter 5

AGENTIC GOVERNANCE

The Confidence Game: When Should Your Agent Act?

Imagine your agent as a new employee. In the beginning, they hesitate. They double-check with a manager before taking action. Over time, as they learn, they handle routine decisions on their own, but still escalate complex or high-risk situations.

Agents follow the same principle, but instead of gut feeling or experience, their autonomy is based on mathematical confidence, derived from how strongly the available data supports a given decision. This allows us to scale trust, not just automation.

Agent confidence is not guesswork, it is scored, logged, and governed. Behind each action sits a calculated probability, often based on:

- the consistency of signal across multiple models (ensemble logic);
- the availability and recency of supporting data;
- the historical reliability of similar past decisions; and
- whether the input falls within the agent's trained domain (vs. out-of-distribution scenarios).

These scores inform three tiers of behavior:

- **High Confidence = Autonomous Action**
  The agent sees enough signal to act. It executes pre-authorized responses, flagging a clear fraud pattern, freezing a compromised account, or generating a low-risk transaction alert. Time is of the essence, and waiting for human input could worsen the outcome.
- **Medium Confidence = Human Partnership**
  The agent sees something abnormal but uncertain. It prepares a summary with contextual markers, prior incidents, known risks, or client history, and routes it to a human reviewer. The agent becomes a decision concierge, not a judge.

- **Low Confidence = Silent Observer**
  Here, the agent lacks strong evidence. It quietly logs the event, perhaps tagging it for pattern analysis later. It contributes to institutional memory without introducing noise or false alarms. This is especially important in edge cases where overreaction can damage client experience.

These tiers are not static. Over time, as agents receive feedback on their actions, accepted decisions, overridden cases, or flagged errors, their confidence models are retrained and thresholds adjusted. This is where governance and learning intersect.

Real-World Application: Confidence in Action

Take Sarah, a retail banking customer. At 2:00 PM, her card is used at a gas station in Chicago. Thirty minutes later, it's charged again, this time at a restaurant in Miami. Your fraud agent detects the geographic impossibility and blocks the Miami charge immediately. This is a high-confidence decision backed by location data, behavioral patterns, and anomaly scoring.

Now imagine Sarah uses her card at a new coffee shop during her usual lunch hour. It's a merchant she's never visited, but the time, location, and amount are consistent with her past behavior. The agent notices the novelty but lets the transaction proceed, logging it as a new behavioral datapoint. That's low-confidence action paired with institutional learning.

Between those extremes sits a gray zone: perhaps Sarah's card is used at a luxury store she's visited before, but the amount is double her average spend. The agent pauses, flags it, and escalates. The decision is not binary; it's collaborative.

This real-time modulation is what separates agentic governance from hardcoded logic. It enables nuance at scale, combining machine judgment with human oversight in a way that evolves daily.

Setting the Right Context

An agent's confidence score is only half the story. The other half is context, the environment in which the decision is made. Just like a human analyst might act differently on a Monday morning versus a holiday weekend, agents must adapt based on customer profile, transaction characteristics, timing, and institutional risk posture.

Contextual governance ensures that agent behavior aligns with business priorities and customer expectations, even when confidence is high.

Let's break this down:

- **Customer Risk Levels Shape Agent Behavior**
  A private banking client expects white-glove service. For these customers, agents operate in a recommendation mode, surfacing insights

and risks for immediate human review, rather than triggering automatic holds. For standard retail clients with predictable behavior patterns, agents can act more autonomously. In both cases, governance is tailored to the relationship tier and associated reputational risk.

- **Transaction Size Matters**
  A $15 coffee flagged incorrectly is an inconvenience. A $15,000 misrouted wire is a crisis. Governance protocols embed risk-weighted thresholds, ensuring that higher-value or higher-impact decisions are escalated even at high confidence. This prevents overreach and limits downside exposure.

- **Time and Place Considerations**
  At 2:00 PM on a Tuesday, an agent can escalate to a human reviewer within minutes. At 2:00 AM on a Sunday, it may need to act alone, blocking a high-risk transaction first, then logging the action for follow-up. Governance includes temporal escalation policies, allowing agents to adapt their behavior based on coverage availability.

- **System Load and Alert Fatigue**
  If human analysts are handling a high volume of alerts, agents may temporarily throttle non-critical escalations, prioritizing only those cases

with high risk or regulatory exposure. This is an institutional fail-safe, ensuring capacity is reserved for the most consequential cases.

Governance isn't just about defining what agents can do; it's about designing when, where, and how they should behave differently across time, clients, and decisions.

Your Governance Framework in Action

To bring this to life, imagine a typical 24-hour cycle inside an institution with multiple agents operating under context-aware, confidence-tiered governance.

- **9:00 AM**
  Your AML agent finishes reviewing overnight alerts. It automatically dismisses 200 low-risk transactions (high confidence, within scope) and escalates 15 edge cases to human analysts now arriving on shift (appropriate context, tiered timing). Governance ensures that no action taken during low-staff windows goes unreviewed.

- **2:00 PM**
  A credit risk agent detects a spike in deposits for a business client. Because this client is classified as high-value, the agent

doesn't adjust limits autonomously, even though the data would permit it. Instead, it escalates to the relationship manager for interpretation. This is governance working across both confidence and client context.

- **11:00 PM**
  A fraud agent detects an account takeover attempt: multiple failed login attempts, IP mismatch, and an unusual device. Despite the late hour, the confidence is high and customer protection protocols grant the agent authority to block access immediately. It then prepares a full event log and schedules customer notification for 8:00 AM.

This multi-agent choreography reflects a mature governance framework, one where each agent understands its boundaries, adapts to context, and contributes to institutional reliability.

Building Institution-Wide Oversight

Governance at the agent level is essential, but as your AI footprint grows, institutional oversight becomes non-negotiable. You're not managing one tool; you're orchestrating a workforce.

Enter the Agent Review Committee, your AI governance council. This body brings together product owners, risk managers, data scientists, compliance officers, and business leaders to serve as the institutional stewards of agent behavior.

Their role isn't just technical, it's strategic. They answer questions like:

- Which agents are safe to scale?
- Where have override frequencies increased, and why?
- Are agent decisions aligning with institutional values and legal expectations?
- When should an agent be paused, retrained, or retired?

The committee becomes your institutional memory and your escalation path. As AI evolves, this team ensures continuity, accountability, and learning across deployments.

Just like new product features require executive sign-off, so should agent autonomy expansions. No agent should silently graduate from assistive to autonomous without a formal review.

Your Control Room Dashboard

Imagine a mission control center, not for spacecraft, but for intelligent agents. In this room, real-time dashboards surface the heartbeat of your agentic ecosystem.

At a glance, you can see:

- Number of decisions made by each agent today
- Escalation rates and override events, segmented by business line

- Bias or fairness indicators across demographics, geographies, or client tiers
- Conflicts between human and agent decisions, and which party was ultimately correct
- Agent drift: when output begins diverging from intended patterns

This is more than observability, it's operational intelligence. The control room allows teams to:
- Detect early signs of governance failure (e.g., rising false positives)
- Preempt regulatory scrutiny with built-in audit trails
- Allocate human review capacity more effectively
- Justify decisions at the board level with data-backed transparency

When integrated across lines of business, this dashboard becomes a shared source of truth, and a cultural artifact that signals accountability.

Making It All Work Together

Modern financial institutions already run dozens, soon hundreds, of agents. Each one might operate under different models, policies, and interfaces. Without consistent governance, this creates fragmentation and risk.

A coherent framework unifies these agents through:

- **Shared Standards**: All agents follow institution-wide ethical guidelines, escalation protocols, and compliance constraints, regardless of their domain.
- **Cross-Agent Awareness**: A fraud agent in retail can signal to a commercial lending agent that a shared client is under investigation. This interconnectedness enables horizontal intelligence, where agents don't act in silos.
- **Audit-Ready Design**: Every agent logs inputs, decisions, outcomes, and overrides. This metadata supports internal reviews and external regulatory requests without disruption.
- **Lifecycle Discipline**: Agents are not fire-and-forget. Each has a defined life cycle: sandbox, pilot, production, review. Like any employee, they need performance reviews and occasionally, offboarding.

This isn't governance as bureaucracy, it's governance as infrastructure. It creates the conditions for trust, scale, and agility to coexist.

Chapter 6

HUMAN + AI: REDEFINING ROLES

W hen Sarah Chen, head of commercial lending, walked into Monday morning's credit committee meeting, she didn't present a single loan file. Instead, she discussed why her AI lending agent had flagged three deals for human override and how those conversations with the agent had revealed blind spots in their risk models that could have cost millions.

This chapter explores what happens when agents become colleagues, answering questions like:

- What decisions should remain human?
- Where do agents lead, and where do they follow?
- How do we design roles, teams, and incentives in a world where intelligence is ambient?

The goal is not to lose control but to gain leverage. When agents handle the repeatable, the pattern-driven, the rules-based tasks, humans can focus on what machines can't: ambiguity, empathy, strategy, and ethics. However, this transition requires redesigning roles from the ground up.

Intelligence Stewardship in Practice

In an agentic institution, managing intelligence is as critical as deploying it. The shift isn't about running systems or chasing alerts; it's about curating a digital workforce that thinks, reasons, and adapts in tandem with the humans it supports. This is where stewardship, orchestration, and trust converge, turning governance into a living discipline rather than a static set of controls.

Building on the architectural foundations and trust by design principles covered in chapter 2, the daily rhythm begins with oversight. Agent Stewards open performance consoles not to inspect dashboards in the old sense, but to review the pulse of institutional intelligence: the volume of automated decisions, the distribution of confidence scores, the frequency of human overrides, and any drift indicators hinting that an agent's reasoning is straying from policy norms. A sudden spike in mid-confidence escalations from a credit agent, for instance, isn't just noise; it's a signal, pointing either to shifting market conditions or to the need for retraining.

Exceptions, once seen as distractions, become design inputs. When an AML agent escalates a case with logic that contradicts prior patterns, the steward follows its reasoning trail, inspects linked evidence, and either validates the escalation or intervenes with documented justification. Each action feeds back into the agent's memory, subtly reshaping its future reasoning. Weekly reviews formalize this cycle. Samples of agent decisions are traced back to their data sources, policy benchmarks are checked for alignment, and misinterpretations of new regulations or market shifts are flagged for retraining. These moments become learning journals, institutional records of how human judgment fine-tunes machine logic over time.

Orchestration and Trust Management

This stewardship, however, is only one dimension of intelligence management. Orchestration designers shape how humans and agents work together, codifying when an agent acts autonomously, when it hands off to a human, and how feedback flows back into its learning loop. In credit underwriting, for example, agents gather data, run policy checks, and draft reasoned proposals, while humans step in to validate nuances or override edge cases. Playbooks formalize these patterns, embedding escalation thresholds, feedback protocols, and predefined handoffs. Before they ever go live, these workflows are rehearsed in sandbox environments, simulating real-world cases and compliance scenarios to ensure they hold up under pressure.

Over time, orchestration matures from process design into adaptive choreography. Logs of human-agent interactions are reviewed monthly to identify bottlenecks: agents that escalate too often, humans intervening unnecessarily, and thresholds that need tuning. Updates follow not in sporadic projects but in steady refinements, keeping the system responsive to shifting conditions. With well-designed orchestration, agents stop being handoff tools and start functioning as colleagues, predictable, accountable, and aligned.

Layered on top of stewardship and orchestration is trust management. This is where ethics and reputation enter operational design. Trust managers continuously monitor fairness indicators, parity metrics across client segments, approval rates by region, and drift away from historical baselines.

When anomalies surface, they drill into reasoning logs and data sources to isolate causes, often uncovering stale inputs or unintended correlations that warrant immediate correction. Quarterly audits expand this lens, comparing current outputs to baselines, assessing policy conformance, and flagging decisions that might invite regulatory scrutiny or reputational harm.

Trust isn't left to passive oversight. It's stress-tested through scenario exercises: feeding agents borderline cases to probe for unintended bias, simulating regulatory changes to watch adaptation, or exploring reputational flashpoints before they happen. When high-stakes cases emerge, a loan denial involving sensitive variables, for instance, trust managers act as circuit breakers, overriding outcomes and documenting rationale for both audit trails and agent retraining. Over time, this loop shifts the function from defensive compliance to proactive trust-building, embedding reputational awareness directly into the intelligence fabric.

Redesigning Work and Teams

These disciplines, stewardship, orchestration, and trust, don't live in isolation. They converge in how work itself is redesigned. In the front office, agents assemble client briefings, surface predictive insights, and capture action items in real time, allowing relationship managers to focus entirely on high-value advisory conversations. In the middle office, agents reconcile records, resolve routine exceptions, and simulate operational contingencies, freeing staff to shift from error-chasing to scenario planning. In risk and compliance, agents filter noise into ranked clusters and deliver fully assembled case packets, enabling analysts to move from queue processing to strategic detection design.

As this model scales, teams reorganize around outcomes rather than functions. Hybrid pods form: cross-functional groups where humans and agents share defined missions. A liquidity pod might pair treasury specialists and risk analysts with a liquidity forecasting agent. A compliance pod might unite AML officers and audit staff with an AML triage agent. Each pod integrates its digital colleagues directly into daily rituals, performance huddles reviewing overnight agent insights, decision clinics dissecting overrides, and retrospectives where both human and agent performance are discussed side by side.

This is also where culture shifts. Ethics scenarios become routine practice rather than isolated training. Leaders visibly query agents in review meetings, modeling curiosity and reinforcing that governance is not just procedural, it's participatory. Performance metrics evolve: teams are rewarded not only for outcomes but for how effectively they refine agent intelligence and improve orchestration quality. Curiosity is formalized into risk control, with "Ask the Agent" sessions institutionalizing the habit of probing reasoning paths, surfacing blind spots before they cascade.

In this environment, agents are not just embedded, they are normalized. They receive performance reviews, sit within team rituals, and contribute visibly to shared goals. Humans don't manage them as tools; they coach them as colleagues. This is what it means to move beyond system management to intelligence stewardship, a model where oversight is active, learning is continuous, and the enterprise itself evolves as a living, adaptive network of human and machine judgment.

Here, intelligence isn't centralized in systems or siloed in departments. It's distributed across an institution that thinks, learns, and aligns in real time, an enterprise where humans scale judgment, agents scale cognition, and together they create an operating model grounded in transparency, trust, and speed.

New Skills for the Agentic Age

Agentic enterprises means redefining what it means to be skilled.

Three foundational skillsets are emerging:
- Orchestration Literacy: Professionals must learn how to work with agents as

collaborators. This includes setting decision boundaries, interpreting output rationales, managing escalations, and curating feedback loops.

- AI Judgment: The ability to assess agent reliability, spot misalignment, and know when to trust or override agent outputs.
- Ethical Reasoning in Action: Embedding ethical reflexes into daily decisions, ensuring fairness, transparency, and accountability.

To support the rise of these new skills, institutions are shifting away from strictly defined roles and fixed performance metrics. Instead of creating jobs with static responsibilities, leading organizations now focus on skill groups: flexible sets of abilities that can be used across different projects as needed. For example, a CX Orchestrator may need three key skills: understanding customer emotions, working smoothly with AI, and knowing company policies. These skill groups make it easier to form teams quickly for new projects and help employees move between different roles.

This hybrid workforce changes how success is measured. No longer based on their individual performance, success metrics look at how well a person improves agent performance, enhances team orchestration, or resolves ambiguity.

Since these performance metrics require adaptability, leaders must incentivize continuous learning, feedback sharing, and experimentation. Some institutions now treat agent performance improvement as a team, reinforcing the idea that agents are teammates to be developed, not just tools to be used.

Together, these changes shift institutional identity: from workforce managers to capability ecosystems, where talent, technology, and trust co-evolve.

Culture, Leadership, and Change

With all these changes in roles, structure, and skills, the culture will naturally shift. Success hinges on having a culture that will allow for these changes.

To have success, you will need these three culture shifts:

- From Ownership to Stewardship: In traditional roles, expertise meant owning decisions end-to-end. In agentic roles, it means stewarding systems that make decisions. This can feel like a loss of control. But leading organizations reframe it as elevation: humans set goals, guide intent, and manage exceptions, enabling the system to scale their judgment.
- From Certainty to Curiosity: When decisions are automated, confidence often depends on understanding what you don't know.

Institutions must foster cultures where asking "What is the agent missing?" or "Where could this go wrong?" is encouraged, not punished. Curiosity becomes a risk control, not a liability.

- From Execution to Exploration: As agents handle repeatable tasks, human time shifts toward ambiguity, design, and innovation. But that shift requires cultural permission. Staff must feel safe experimenting, offering feedback, and challenging system behavior, not just executing what's scripted.

In order for the culture to change, the leaders must:

- Model the New Mindset: Executives must demonstrate what it means to work with agents: asking for rationale, sharing override decisions, and discussing agent performance as they would a team member's. These visible behaviors normalize human and AI collaboration, turning it from a pilot project into a leadership principle.
- Codify Institutional Rituals: Leaders must ensure the institution has regular agent performance reviews where teams reflect on decision quality and alignment. Their role is to override debriefs, share judgment calls, refine escalation logic, and prepare learning

logs, capturing how humans taught agents, reinforcing the value of collaboration.

- Tell the Right Stories: Nothing moves culture like narrative. Institutions that lead in agentic adoption must share stories of partnership, not displacement. As they shape the narrative, leaders must spotlight the relationship manager who used an agent to deepen a client bond, not the one who automated a task away.

With the right incentives, structures, and symbols, agentic transformation becomes not just accepted but embraced.

The Human Dividend

In the end, the promise of agentic systems goes beyond efficiency. It's a more human-centered enterprise, where machines handle the routine, and people rise to the meaningful.

This human dividend is the value unlocked when agents absorb repetition, process complexity, and surface insights.

Humans now spend less time navigating systems and more time navigating outcomes. They move from "what happened" to "what matters." From clicks to context. From status updates to strategic action.

And because of this, client interactions become deeper, not just faster. When agents handle logistics, professionals can focus on empathy, nuance, and advisory trust, the intangibles that create enduring relationships.

The human dividend is measurable. Relationship managers spend X more time in advisory conversations. Risk analysts shift from processing X cases daily to designing detection systems that prevent thousands of incidents. Compliance officers move from chasing violations to preventing them.

Ultimately, agentic banking means amplifying humans by creating organizations where every role, team, and outcome is better than what we could achieve alone.

Chapter 7

AGENTIC INFRASTRUCTURE: SYSTEMS THAT LEARN AND ACT

R ecent digital transformations have typically been platform-centric, focusing on centralizing data, modernizing infrastructure, and streamlining delivery. While these platforms made banking faster, agentic systems require a different foundation that serves users and has an infrastructure that supports autonomous intelligence.

Where traditional systems wait for input, agentic infrastructure supports systems that initiate action. That means infrastructure must do more than route messages or store data. It must:
- Enable persistent intelligence that learns from experience
- Support low-latency decision-making at scale
- Connect seamlessly across silos, partners, and policies

In short, infrastructure thus evolves from passive plumbing to a cognitive substrate, the environment in which digital agents live, learn, and operate.

The Agentic Intelligence Stack

Agentic banking requires an infrastructure that brings together interconnected, cognitive components.
The core layer includes:
- Data Layer: This is where everything starts. But unlike traditional data warehouses, the agentic data layer must be event-driven and real-time, continuously refreshed, and linked across sources. It also needs to be contextual and semantic, enabling agents to operate with understanding, not just numbers.
- Model Layer: At this level, agents gain cognition. Models perform tasks like prediction, classification, anomaly detection, and recommendation. But in agentic systems, models are not static

APIs. They need to be composable, monitored, and aligned. This means models need to adapt to context, be governed for bias and drive, and serve institutional objectives.

- Orchestration Layer: Here, intelligence becomes action. The orchestration layer determines which agent should act, manages adaptation and escalation, and embeds oversight.
- Agent Layer: This is where intelligence becomes operational. Agents act autonomously based on context, rules, and memory, aligning behavior with institutional policy.
- Governance & Observability Layer: At the top of the stack sits the layer that ensures alignment and safety. It includes access control, audit trails, transparency, and real-time performance monitoring.

What emerges from this stack is a new kind of infrastructure, where agents become living, adaptive parts of the organization, able to evolve alongside the institution.

Data as a live asset

The foundation of this stack begins with transforming how we think about data itself. In traditional systems, data is treated like a warehouse, stored, queried, and reported in batches. In agentic systems, data becomes something else entirely: a live asset.

This transformation requires three foundational shifts:

- From Storage to Stream: Data must be event-driven, captured as it happens, processed as it arrives, and acted upon without delay.
- From Schema to Semantics: Data must be tagged, contextualized, and semantically modeled, allowing agents to reason and discover relationships.
- From Control to Collaboration: Governance remains strong, but access and policies are embedded into data pipelines to empower responsible agent autonomy.

Once these foundational shifts are in play, you'll need technical capabilities to realize data as a live asset, such as event-driven architecture, contextual memory, and data provenance.

For Lisa, this means her treasury agents can detect a liquidity pattern emerging across Asian markets and immediately correlate it with pending European settlements, all without waiting for overnight batch processing. Rather than polling for changes, agentic systems subscribe to event streams: a credit anomaly, a sudden liquidity shift, a client behavior change; each triggers alerts, escalations, or autonomous action. This reduces latency, enabling agents to respond and adapt instantly rather than reacting to outdated snapshots.

Live data must persist in meaningfully linked context. Agents require memory to track interaction histories, resolutions applied, and evolving patterns over time.

This enables personalization, consistency, and continuous learning across workflows.

Data moving through the system carries its lineage and permissions with it. Smart pipelines embed policy directly into data flows, so agents know what data they can use, how to justify decisions, and who can override actions.

Together, these capabilities transform infrastructure from passive recordkeeping to a robust, adaptive nervous system.

Real-Time Decisioning at Scale

In traditional banking systems, decisions are made in scheduled batches and often held for manual review. Approvals, fraud checks, and risk adjustments happen hours or even days after the triggering event. In an agentic bank, this paradigm disappears. Decision-making becomes continuous and decentralized, unfolding in real time across thousands of micro-judgments that ripple through the enterprise.

When Lisa's agents detect unusual FX volatility, they instantly adjust hedging positions, notify relevant stakeholders, and document their reasoning, all within milliseconds.

Micro-Decisions, Macro-Impact

Agentic systems deconstruct large processes into millisecond-scale judgments:

- Should this transaction proceed?
- Is this client profile consistent with its historical behavior?
- Does this risk threshold need to be adjusted in light of market volatility?

Each decision is logged, timestamped, and linked to its evidence base, creating a traceable decision fabric where every micro-action builds institutional memory.

To support this, institutions must invest in event-driven infrastructure. Event streaming platforms such as Apache Kafka, Confluent Cloud, or AWS Kinesis serve as the backbone, propagating decisions and state changes instantly across systems and agents. For banks operating at scale, tens of millions of daily events, this requires throughput in the range of millions of events per second and low-latency messaging measured in milliseconds, not seconds.

Policy-Embedded Logic

In a real-time environment, agents cannot pause for approvals. Institutional intent must be embedded into their reasoning. This involves:

- Encoding compliance rules directly into decision workflows using policy engines (e.g., Open Policy Agent or Azure Policy) that reference regulatory, risk, and ethical constraints.
- Integrating data lineage tools such as Apache Atlas, Collibra, or Alation to ensure every decision is auditable back to its inputs.
- Maintaining version-controlled policy libraries that adapt dynamically to regulatory updates while retaining historic auditability.

This is how agents make instantaneous decisions without drifting outside governance boundaries.

Scalable Compute Infrastructure

Agents need instant access to processing power. Traditional shared compute or nightly batch processing won't suffice. Banks are now moving toward cloud-native, GPU-accelerated infrastructure that can handle thousands of parallel inferences simultaneously.

- For small-scale deployments (e.g., 50–100 agents in targeted use cases), 8–16 GPUs (NVIDIA A100 or H100-class) across a managed Kubernetes cluster are sufficient for sub-second inference.
- For enterprise-scale agent networks (hundreds of agents processing real-time transactions), configurations may require 50+ GPUs across

distributed nodes with autoscaling in cloud environments such as AWS (SageMaker + EKS), Azure Machine Learning, or Google Vertex AI.
- Memory requirements typically range from 50–100 TB of high-speed storage for agent memory, decision logs, and lineage tracking, often backed by services like Snowflake or Databricks with tiered object storage on AWS S3 or Azure Blob.

Cost Implications: At scale, running real-time decision infrastructure can cost several million dollars annually, driven by GPU utilization, high-frequency storage reads/writes, and event streaming throughput. However, when benchmarked against traditional operational overhead (manual reviews, delays, losses from fraud or missed opportunities), real-time decisioning often delivers a 3–5x ROI in efficiency gains and risk reduction.

Coordinated autonomy and shared state

Continuous decisioning only works if agents share situational awareness. This requires:
- Broadcasting state changes through event streams (e.g., an AML agent notifying a payments agent that a transaction is under review).
- Priority queues and orchestration engines (e.g., Temporal, Cadence) to ensure urgent signals, like sanctions matches, preempt lower-priority tasks.

- Inter-agent protocols built on lightweight messaging (MQTT, gRPC) to synchronize context across domains in milliseconds.

When ambiguity arises, such as conflicting risk signals, agents must have automatic fallback paths to humans-in-the-loop, routing cases to stewards or analysts through integrated explainability consoles.

The Real-Time Operating Model

This is not simply technology; it's a shift in how decisions live inside the bank. Event-driven compute, GPU-backed inference, embedded policy logic, and coordinated autonomy create an environment where agents act in milliseconds, align in real time, and defer gracefully when judgment is needed.

In this model, the infrastructure doesn't just run the bank, it thinks with it.

System Interoperability and Strategic APIs

Effective agentic systems rely on interoperability. Agents must access core systems, trigger workflows, and receive up-to-date context.

This comes through APIs:
- Contextual APIs: Standardized, secure interfaces that expose not only data but also intent. For example, they don't just get an

account balance but verify liquidity sufficiency for FX trade. These APIs allow agents to act purposefully, not blindly.

- Composable APIs: APIs can be reusable across use cases, describe what should happen, and be discoverable and searchable.
- Governed APIs: Role-based permissions, audit trails, and policy enforcement are necessary to make APIs strategic, trustworthy assets.

Advanced design patterns, such as intent meshes (where agents dynamically publish goals and subscribe to others) and process digital twins (which codify workflows for agent alignment), extend this flexibility, ensuring agents do not act in isolation but operate as coordinated digital colleagues.

Building Your Agentic Infrastructure: A Phased Approach

Transforming to agentic infrastructure doesn't happen overnight. Most institutions should prioritize:
- Phase 1: Event-driven data architecture and real-time streaming
- Phase 2: Model deployment and orchestration capabilities
- Phase 3: Advanced agent coordination and autonomous decision-making

- Phase 4: Full interoperability and ecosystem integration

Infrastructure as a Strategic Asset

In a platform-centric world, infrastructure enables operations. In an agentic world, infrastructure determines competitive advantage. Institutions compete on how well their systems think, learn, and act autonomously, ethically, and at scale.

Your infrastructure determines how smart your bank can be. For Lisa, our treasury executive, this forms the bedrock of her entire operation. Her agents run forecasts, interpret liquidity shocks, simulate regulatory impacts, and adjust exposures across time zones in real time. Without infrastructure supporting low-latency computation, composable services, and scalable learning, none of this would be possible.

Chapter 8

TREASURY AS A COGNITIVE SYSTEM

L isa's mornings used to be defined by static dashboards and delayed reports. Forecasts reflected what had already happened, funding actions lagged behind reality, and unexpected disruptions often triggered emergency borrowing.

Now, her treasury is different. It's no longer reactive, it's alive. Her liquidity agents sense market movements as they happen, simulate intraday funding scenarios, and propose actions in real time. Instead of waiting for overnight batches, Lisa gets recommendations, complete with reasoning trails and confidence scores, that compress decision-making from days to seconds.

It didn't happen overnight. The transformation began with a single use case, automating overnight liquidity alerts, and evolved into an entire agentic ecosystem that monitors, simulates, and optimizes liquidity across time zones. What started as a reactive control layer has become a cognitive partner.

This is no longer just treasury automation. It's treasury cognition.

How Multisource Perception Works

Lisa's agents continuously ingest streams of data from multiple sources:

- **ERP Systems** (e.g., SAP, Oracle): Accounts payable and receivable positions, projected settlements.
- **Banking APIs**: Payment flows from SWIFT gpi and Fedwire, intraday balances from core banking.
- **Market Feeds**: FX rates, funding spreads, and bond yields from Bloomberg or Refinitiv.

- **External Signals**: Weather forecasts (NOAA), supply chain disruption alerts, and geopolitical event trackers.

By blending these signals, the agents uncover correlations that static systems miss. For example, they've learned that severe weather in certain supplier regions historically delays cash inflows, increasing short-term liquidity risk.

What makes this possible is the shift from linear ingestion to compositional reasoning. Traditional systems treated each data source as siloed input; agents use attention models and vector embeddings to assess not just the source, but its relevance and interaction with other variables. A drop in expected receivables doesn't mean the same thing during quiet markets versus when FX volatility spikes. The agent can weigh those signals differently in real time.

These agents also access institutional memory, stored as vectorized event histories. When a disruption occurs, they search for similar patterns across thousands of previous events, not by keyword, but by meaning. "Have we seen this before? What worked last time? What failed?"

This memory isn't just a lookup table, it's contextual. For instance, during a past liquidity crunch triggered by sudden oil price movements, a treasury agent learned to cross-reference exposure to energy suppliers with payment term shifts. That learning becomes embedded in future simulations.

System Architecture Overview

Lisa's cognitive treasury system is built like a three-story building, where each floor has a specific job.

Ground Floor, Data Collection

Think of this as a giant funnel that never stops working. Banking systems, market feeds, and ERP platforms constantly send information through secure connections, like having dozens of dedicated phone lines that never hang up. When a payment clears in Tokyo or currency rates shift in London, the system knows within seconds, not hours.

This data layer is built on event-driven pipelines and stream processing infrastructure, using tools like Kafka, Flink, or cloud-native equivalents. These platforms enable agents to process transactions, market movements, and operational events as they occur, not in batch windows.

Each data type is tagged by source, reliability, and latency sensitivity, so agents can prioritize high-confidence, low-lag inputs when making split-second decisions. A Treasury API feed might be trusted more than an external news sentiment alert when funding decisions are urgent.

To ensure composability, Lisa's team uses a semantic data layer, a unified treasury ontology that maps incoming data to consistent meaning: a payable is a payable, no matter its system of origin.

This standardization allows agents to reason across ERP silos, geographies, and third-party data.

Second Floor, Pattern Recognition

This is where the magic happens. The system has learned from thousands of past decisions, market events, and outcomes. It spots patterns humans might miss, like noticing that supplier payments from Vietnam typically slow down 72 hours before weather alerts, or that certain currency movements predict funding spread changes. It's constantly asking "What does this remind me of?" and "What usually happens next?"

This layer is powered by retrieval-augmented generation (RAG) models, which combine real-time querying of treasury history with large language models fine-tuned on financial patterns. These agents don't just recall past events, they contextualize them. They understand that a 50 basis point spread widening during Fed week is different than during a geopolitical crisis.

Agents apply temporal pattern recognition, looking for lead-lag relationships and structural anomalies. For example:

- A supplier delay three times in a quarter triggers a predictive shortfall flag.
- An FX volatility spike tied to specific counterparties prompts auto-risk exposure recalculations.

This layer integrates with simulation engines to run what-if scenarios across multiple balance sheets, currencies, and timelines, allowing for proactive rather than reactive actions.

Third Floor, Decision-Making

Here's where recommendations get made. Every suggestion comes with a confidence score and clear reasoning: "I'm 89% confident you should hedge this FX exposure because similar patterns in the past led to $2.5M losses when left unhedged."

The system knows Lisa's rules and won't recommend anything outside her authority limits without flagging it for approval.

But this floor does more than just suggest. It:

- Tracks Lisa's personal decision style (e.g., risk tolerance, typical overrides) and tailors recommendations accordingly.
- Classifies decisions into assistive, actionable, or delegable, aligning with internal governance tiers.
- Records every output into a chain-of-reasoning log, ensuring every treasury action has a transparent audit trail.

The decision layer is integrated with execution systems: payments, FX desks, and credit lines. Lisa can authorize directly from the agent's dashboard, every action logged with timestamp, rationale, and agent ID.

Scenario 1: Weather-Linked Liquidity Stress

On Lisa's console, a typhoon alert flashes from the NOAA API. Her agents immediately connect it to ERP payables linked to Vietnamese suppliers and historical payment delay data.

  Data Flow:
  - **Weather Feed**: Typhoon forecast detected in the supplier region
  - **ERP**: $15M in pending receivables tied to impacted suppliers
  - **Historical Memory**: Past typhoons caused an average 3–4 day delay in this corridor
  - **Banking APIs**: Tokyo branch operating with marginal liquidity buffer

  Agent Response:
  - **Detect**: Link environmental signals with supplier-level cash flow projections
  - **Simulate**: Run scenario of delayed receivables against current outflows
  - **Coordinate**: Alert global liquidity agent to assess coverage across other branches
  - **Recommend**: Transfer $10M from Frankfurt surplus to Tokyo (confidence: 92%)

Escalation Logic:
- Action requires Lisa's approval due to policy limit on interregional preemptive transfers
- Lisa reviews the simulation dashboard, sees expected coverage dip, and approves
- Funds are moved ahead of impact, avoiding overdraft triggers and short-term facility drawdowns

Agent Roles in Scenario 1

Agent Type	Role	Decision Scope
Environmental Monitor	Detect typhoon risk	Alert-only
Receivables Agent	Simulate delay exposure	Advisory
Global Liquidity Agent	Optimize branch balances	Recommend + Execute

Scenario 2: Market Volatility and FX Hedging

Minutes later, market feeds register sudden yen appreciation.

Data Flow:
- **Market Feed**: FX rate spike detected (JPY/USD)
- **Treasury Ledger**: $200M exposure flagged for end-of-day conversion
- **Agent Memory**: Historical patterns link yen surges with widening swap spreads

- **ERP Forecasts**: Large vendor payments expected next week in USD

Agent Response:
- **Detect**: Identify FX mismatch exposure under stressed conditions
- **Simulate**: Project conversion loss under +1% FX shift → $2.5M loss
- **Recommend**: Enter forward hedge (confidence: 89%)

Execution:
- Lisa authorizes trade within agent's dashboard
- Trade is executed via linked FX desk interface
- Agent logs the decision rationale, timestamp, and confirmation trail for audit

Cross-Agent Impact:

The FX hedging agent also notifies the risk aggregation agent, which recalculates the firm's composite VaR (value at risk) based on the hedge. The update propagates to capital planning dashboards, ensuring consistency across treasury and risk functions.

Scenario 3: Intraday Liquidity Balancing

Later in the day, Fedwire settlement data shows unexpected outflows from the New York branch while Frankfurt posts a surplus.

Data Flow:
- **Banking API**: NYC branch liquidity dips post high-value settlement
- **ERP**: Frankfurt reports €12M surplus from receivables
- **Historical Agent Logs**: Intrabranch transfers consistently save 15–20 bps vs. credit drawdown

Agent Response:
- **Detect**: Identify emerging mismatch at NYC
- **Simulate**: Cost of drawing on credit line vs. internal transfer
- **Recommend**: Shift €12M from Frankfurt to NYC immediately

Execution:
- Transfer falls within Lisa's predefined thresholds
- Agent executes without escalation
- Action is logged with settlement timestamp and funding impact delta

Intraday Optimization Metrics

Metric	Credit Line Draw	Internal Transfer
Estimated Cost (bps)	32	12
Execution Delay (mins)	10	2
Governance Threshold	>$5M, <1hr delay	Auto-Approved

Treasury as a Living System

Through these connected flows, Lisa's treasury now anticipates disruptions rather than reacting to them. The agents don't just warn her about risks; they calculate the best move, explain why, and act when approved.

This isn't automation. It's cognition. And like any living system, Lisa's treasury now demonstrates three critical characteristics:

1. Perception with Memory

Agents don't see events in isolation. Each new datapoint, an FX spike, a delayed receivable, a political headline, is understood in the context of past occurrences. Just as the human brain links smell to memory, these agents associate signals across time, source, and scenario. The treasury doesn't just remember numbers, it remembers patterns.

This memory is dynamic and self-prioritizing. For example, if a bond auction coincides with volatility spikes three out of the last five cycles, the system tags that as a conditional pattern worth weighting in future simulations.

2. Decision with Restraint

Treasury agents aren't designed to replace human judgment. They're built to know their limits. Each operates within scoped decision boundaries:
- **Monitor agents** flag anomalies
- **Advisor agents** simulate and recommend
- **Executor agents** act only under pre-cleared thresholds

These categories are not static. A monitor agent may graduate to advisor status after months of correct alerts. Conversely, an executor agent may be throttled back if false positives increase. This creates a performance-based authority model, mirroring how human analysts grow or narrow their scope.

3. Behavior with Coherence

The system behaves like an institution, not a stack of tools. When one agent identifies a funding anomaly, others adjust exposure logic, capital forecasts, or alerts. This cross-agent signaling prevents siloed decisions and enables what treasury has long needed: systemic coordination at machine speed.

Example: When the FX hedging agent executes a large forward contract, it doesn't operate in isolation. It triggers a VaR recalculation by the risk aggregation agent, which in turn prompts the capital planning agent to adjust buffers for stress testing. This isn't one decision; it's a sequence of interoperable actions aligned to institutional objectives.

For Lisa, this means fewer emergencies, tighter funding control, and a treasury function that operates at market speed while staying firmly under human oversight. Treasury has become what it was always meant to be: a forward-looking engine of stability and advantage.

Beyond Liquidity: Risk, Funding, and Capital Strategy

The same agentic principles powering Lisa's liquidity optimization extend across broader treasury functions, especially in risk management, funding execution, and capital strategy. These domains have long been governed by spreadsheet models, committee approvals, and delayed data. In the agentic model, they become continuous, context-aware, and simulation-driven.

Risk Agents: From Limits to Active Sensing

Traditional treasury risk management relies on policy thresholds and quarterly stress tests. Risk agents transform this into an active, always-on capability.

Core Functions:
- Continuously scan for mismatches between policy limits and live market behavior
- Recalculate exposure every time conditions shift (e.g., FX, credit, counterparty, political risk)
- Connect macro volatility with micro-exposures (e.g., local lending tied to global FX flows)

Examples in Action:
- A hedging agent notices that the notional coverage ratio for a major currency position has slipped below 0.85 due to new inflows. It recommends rolling forward contracts and simulates impact under three volatility paths.
- A counterparty risk agent downgrades an internal exposure to a regional bank after detecting a negative sentiment trend across filings, analyst calls, and sovereign risk indices. It advises internal credit line tightening and cross-links to liquidity buffers.

These agents operate with tiered authority: they act directly on portfolio rebalancing under preset thresholds, and escalate when strategic thresholds or board-facing limits are in play.

Funding Agents: From Scheduling to Opportunistic Refinancing

Funding strategies were once static, set quarterly, reviewed monthly, and executed manually. Funding agents make treasury funding adaptive, opportunistic, and margin-sensitive.

Core Functions:
- Monitor market windows for optimal funding cost (intraday, overnight, long-term)
- Reprice options based on cost of capital, tax arbitrage, behavioral prepayment likelihood
- Propose refinancing or debt scheduling changes in real-time

Examples in Action:
- A funding agent observes that cross-currency basis swaps between USD and EUR have narrowed by 40 bps, creating a low-cost window for short-term borrowing in EUR. It recommends a $200M refinancing, factoring tax advantages for the firm's Luxembourg entity.
- Another agent notices early loan prepayment behavior among corporate clients and suggests pulling forward a funding tranche to take advantage of favorable cash flow positioning.

These agents rely on a composite optimization model, balancing cost, timing, regulatory treatment, and strategic liquidity reserves. They reduce the opportunity cost of inertia by identifying margin opportunities as soon as they arise.

Capital Strategy Agents: From Compliance to Simulation

Capital planning has long centered on compliance: buffer requirements, ICAAP processes, and regulatory disclosures. But capital is also a strategic asset. Agentic systems treat it as such.

Core Functions:
- Simulate capital adequacy under macro and micro stress scenarios
- Reallocate surplus or cushion buffers across entities based on real-time balance sheet health
- Support board discussions, ICAAP filings, and regulatory tests with forward-facing views

Examples in Action:
- A capital agent runs a live simulation: "If FX volatility persists for 10 days at this level, what's the impact on our Basel III capital ratio?" It finds that an early hedge could save 22 bps in regulatory capital impact and recommends action.

- During stress planning, another agent models systemic shocks: what happens if both counterparty exposures and market funding spreads spike simultaneously? Results are visualized and handed to the CRO and CFO with action thresholds.

These agents become co-pilots for capital stewards, not replacing regulation, but adding a living layer of foresight to capital strategy.

Reframing Treasury's Role

The treasury function is no longer just about managing liquidity, it's about orchestrating foresight. As institutions embed agents into risk, funding, and capital decisions, treasury becomes the connective tissue between finance, operations, and strategy.

Lisa doesn't just respond faster; she leads with precision. Her agents don't eliminate human judgment, they elevate it. They surface insights before spreadsheets catch up. They simulate scenarios before crises emerge. And they coordinate across silos before organizational inertia sets in.

This is treasury in the agentic era:
- Perceptive, not passive
- Strategic, not segmented
- Adaptive, not reactive

The real value isn't in automation, it's in orchestration. Not in replacing people, but in amplifying them. Treasury is no longer a back-office control function. It's a front-line command center for enterprise resilience.

And as more CFOs and treasurers adopt this model, they won't just see fewer overdrafts or better funding costs. They'll unlock a new kind of institutional intelligence, one that senses, simulates, and steers in real time.

Because when treasury becomes cognitive, the whole institution moves faster, with more confidence, and with clarity.

Chapter 9

CLIENT EXPERIENCE AT MACHINE SPEED

n most banks, client experience remains reactive. Onboarding takes days. Requests flow through manual queues. Relationship managers rely on gut instinct and fragmented data. The result: inconsistent service, missed opportunities, and growing friction.

These intelligent systems learn what each client needs and act on it before being asked.

For Lisa, this change affects her internal clients (product, risk, and markets) who now interact with client experience agents that detect shifts in behavior, proactively surface opportunities or risks and engage users in natural language, resolving issues or escalating when needed.

Externally, agents guide clients through onboarding steps in real time, pre-fill forms based on known data, and answer complex product questions using live documentation and policy-based RAG systems.

Three layers of transformation drive this shift:

- Persistent Client Context: Agents maintain memory of prior interactions, preferences, and goals. This continuity enables nuanced personalization without asking the client to repeat themselves.
- Multimodal Interaction: Clients engage through chat, voice, embedded widgets, whatever fits the moment. Large Language Models (LLM) translate unstructured queries into structured action, while RAG ensures answers are grounded in institutional knowledge.
- Action-Oriented Design: Agents execute, opening accounts, updating instructions, triggering compliance flows, always within governed boundaries.

Relationship Manager and Agent Collaboration

The role of the relationship manager is transforming. No longer burdened by reactive service tasks or manual CRM updates, RMs now work alongside a mesh of client experience (CX) agents that track sentiment shifts, detect behavioral anomalies, and propose proactive engagement strategies, complete with context, talking points, and tailored offers.

Instead of scanning static profiles or waiting for client escalations, RMs start their day reviewing live, intelligent briefings generated by their agents.

A Morning in Context

Aisha, a senior RM covering high-value commercial clients in Europe, the Middle East, and Africa (EMEA), begins her day with her CX agent's dashboard:

CX Agent: "Client: NovaTech Holdings. Sentiment trend: declining. Communication analysis detected neutral-to-negative phrasing in last two calls ('concerned about delays'). Behavioral cue: reduced FX transaction volume (-15% over 2 weeks). Suggested action: proactive outreach. Talking points: delivery timelines, hedging support. Confidence: 86%."

Aisha opens the details, scanning the reasoning path: client transcripts parsed by NLP, transaction data sourced from treasury logs, and historical patterns comparing similar accounts.

Interactive dialogue: Override in action

Aisha clicks "Engage" but chooses to adjust the recommendation.

Aisha: "Override: Delay outreach until after scheduled board meeting on Thursday. Rationale: Client hinted last week they're waiting on internal approvals."

CX Agent: "Acknowledged. Override logged. Adjusting outreach window to Friday morning. Would you like me to prepare updated talking points aligned with post-board scenarios?"

Aisha: "Yes, include two scenarios: one if they approve expansion, another if they defer. Use prior expansion case notes from 2022 as reference."

CX Agent: "Understood. Drafting scenario-specific engagement briefs now. Incorporating 2022 expansion precedent and aligning to current FX positions."

A Second Dialogue: Rejecting a Misaligned Recommendation

Later that afternoon, the CX agent flags another client:

CX Agent: "Client: Helios Manufacturing. Detected risk signals include slowed payment cycles and increased customer support escalations. Sentiment score: low. Suggested action: escalate retention offer with preferential loan terms. Confidence: 78%."

Aisha frowns. She knows Helios's CFO personally and recalls a private conversation last week: their delayed payments were due to a system migration, not financial distress. Offering retention incentives here would not only be premature but also potentially undermine the client's trust.

Aisha: "Reject recommendation. Rationale: Payment delays tied to ERP migration, confirmed directly with the CFO. No retention offer needed, focus instead on support for migration impact."

CX Agent: "Rejection logged. Noted contextual factor: ERP migration (non-financial delay cause). Would you like me to shift the engagement strategy to operational support and product advisory?"

Aisha: "Yes. Prepare a call agenda focused on integration support. No pricing concessions."

CX Agent: "Confirmed. Retention offer removed. Engagement refocused on migration assistance. Updating reasoning weights: payment delays reclassified as operational in the context of confirmed ERP event."

Continuous Learning and Governance

These adjustments don't just solve today's cases, they shape tomorrow's intelligence. Every override, rejection, and note feeds back into the agent's learning system. If multiple RMs log similar feedback, flagging ERP migrations as non-financial delays, for example, the agent re-weights those signals globally, reducing false alerts across the network.

Over time, experience quality metrics track outcomes: time-to-resolution shortens, intervention rates decline, and recommendations become increasingly precise. Segment-level optimization emerges too: what triggers retention offers in mid-market manufacturing differs from what drives outreach in global enterprise finance.

In this co-orchestration model, agents handle sensing, pattern recognition, and synthesis, while humans bring context, judgment, and empathy. Every interaction is both an operational decision and a learning event, blending automation with oversight into a continuously improving system.

Aisha closes her laptop. Today, she didn't just manage clients. She helped train a system that will be smarter tomorrow, one where every interaction sharpens intelligence, reinforces compliance, and deepens trust across the enterprise.

Chapter 10

TRUST, RISK, AND GOVERNANCE AT SCALE

A s agents begin to reason, act, and learn across enterprise functions, the stakes shift. What was once a compliance framework becomes a strategic foundation for scale. Trust, risk, and governance (TRG) are what make AI possible.

Lisa's organization learned this early. As her treasury and CX agents gained autonomy, new questions emerged: What if an agent makes the wrong decision? How is accountability assigned? Can we explain and audit each step of its reasoning?

The old answers, logs, rules, and approvals no longer suffice. In an agentic system, governance must be dynamic, contextual, and layered.

Strategic Imperatives for Agentic TRG

- Embedded Policy Scaffolding: Every agent operates within embedded controls: decision boundaries, risk appetite rules, and regulatory triggers. These are part of the agent's reasoning process from the start. Governance becomes built-in, not bolted-on.
- Explainability by Design: Every action taken, or not taken, by an agent must be explainable to regulators, auditors, and humans. This requires traceable inference paths, data provenance tracking, and natural language justifications. Agents must justify and document their reasoning with clarity and context.
- Human-in-the-Loop Oversight: Some trust must remain human. Override systems, ethical review councils, and scenario audits give humans the power to intervene, pause, or refine agentic behavior.

With these imperatives, governance becomes an enabler of trust at machine scale.

From periodic oversight to continuous assurance

Traditional governance models were designed for systems that waited. Agentic systems perceive, reason, and act, often in milliseconds. Instead of checking up on systems quarterly, you need to watch them every second.

Lisa's organization implemented a layered architecture:

Real-Time Policy Enforcement: Instead of checking compliance post-facto, agents operate within policy-aware execution environments. Every action, from liquidity adjustment to client messaging, is evaluated before it occurs: Does it align with current risk posture? Is it within user authorization? Has it triggered any compliance thresholds?

This creates pre-decision validation, not just post-decision auditing.

Zero Trust Architectures for Agents: Trust is never implicit. Every request, data access, or workflow initiation is verified based on identity, context, role, and risk. Lisa's agents don't just have access, they earn it, action by action.

Governance as Code: Governance is encoded into machine-readable rules: jurisdictional constraints, product eligibility, and client-specific caveats. These are exposed to agents through APIs, RAG-based retrieval layers, or embedded policy agents.

By building governance into the execution path rather than around it, institutions create trust at velocity. Every action is aligned with oversight, every outcome is traceable, and every error is contained before it scales.

Risk Models in the Age of Intelligence

Risk models were once static constructs, updated quarterly and embedded in spreadsheets. Agentic systems operate in real time and demand risk models that do too. Risk becomes a living system.

In Lisa's treasury, the old Value at Risk (VaR) models are still present, but now they're augmented by agents that ingest new variables continuously, adjust exposure profiles dynamically, and simulate not just probable outcomes, but emergent scenarios.

These become reasoned anticipations, driven by models that adapt as the environment evolves.

Three characteristics define agentic risk models:
- Dynamic Variable Ingestion: Risk agents pull from both structured and unstructured sources, ERP feeds, trading signals, regulatory updates, even social sentiment, turning weak signals into early warnings. The model evolves with the context.
- Real-Time Sensitivity Rebalancing: As external conditions change, model weights adjust. During high inflation, interest rate sensitivity rises. During geopolitical unrest, counterparty risk climbs. These shifts are learned

by agents, validated by oversight teams, and monitored through transparent dashboards.

- Explainable Probabilistic Reasoning: Every adjustment or prediction includes a confidence score, rationale, and policy alignment check. Lisa sees not just a warning, but why it emerged, what's likely next, and how it fits treasury's current tolerance.

Risk is understood through collaboration between models, agents, and humans.

For decades, compliance officers were the cleanup crew of banking. Problems were spotted after they happened, reports were written about what went wrong, and new rules were added to prevent repeats. Compliance lived in the past, always playing defense.

That approach is now obsolete. When agents make thousands of micro-decisions per second and market conditions shift by the minute, you can't rely on checklists or policies drafted last quarter. "Catch it later" no longer works.

Lisa's bank flipped the script. Instead of compliance as the department that says no, they embedded compliance logic directly into the decisioning fabric of their institution. Every agent, whether it's in treasury, client service, or risk, operates inside a policy-aware environment that evaluates each action against live regulatory rules before it's ever taken.

Embedded Compliance: From Reaction to Proactive

How Embedded Compliance Logic Works

Picture this: Lisa's treasury agent receives an instruction to move $50 million from Tokyo to London. In the past, this would clear execution first, then show up in a compliance officer's queue for review days later. Now, a compliance agent evaluates it in real time, before it happens.

Here's the actual decision pathway:

Step 1: Sanctions and Watchlists Check

- Agent queries live sanctions databases (e.g., OFAC, UK HMT, EU consolidated list) using RAG-based retrieval.
- If any entity involved matches, it triggers an immediate Level 3 hold and escalation with documented rationale.

Step 2: Jurisdictional Threshold Rules

- Cross-references jurisdictional reporting thresholds (e.g., Japan's Foreign Exchange and Foreign Trade Act, UK PRA liquidity reporting).
- Transaction flagged if it exceeds regulatory thresholds requiring pre-clearance or reporting, e.g., >¥5 billion outbound transfer.
- Outcome: pause and request authorization from Lisa or compliance if over threshold.

Step 3: AML Pattern Detection
- Runs anomaly detection against historical transaction graph: unusual counterparty behavior, round-trip flows, or split-transaction patterns.
- Confidence scoring:
  - » 95% suspicious → automatic freeze + compliance escalation
  - » 80–94% unusual → flag for review with supporting rationale
  - » <80% → log to institutional memory for monitoring

Step 4: Tax and Reporting Compliance
- Checks whether transfer creates tax-reportable event across involved jurisdictions (e.g., UK HMRC or Japanese NTA requirements).
- If triggered, auto-prepares filing packet for compliance queue while holding execution until confirmation.

Step 5: Conflict-of-Interest and Internal Limits
- Evaluates exposure against internal counterparty concentration limits and risk appetite statements stored in policy-as-code.
- If exceeded, routes for approval by the treasury head plus compliance.

Sometimes the rules collide. For instance:

- A transfer is permissible under AML and sanctions screening, but breaches an internal liquidity concentration limit.
- The agent must weigh institutional risk appetite (internal limit breach) against regulatory clearance (no legal breach).

Here's how it handles it:

- Regulatory rules always take precedence; transactions violating law or sanctions stop instantly.
- Internal risk or policy limits trigger tiered escalation: the agent generates a conditional approval path requiring explicit sign-off from treasury leadership and compliance before proceeding.

In Lisa's case, the compliance agent presented her with a decision panel:

Agent Output:

> "Transaction cleared under AML and sanctions. Internal liquidity concentration limit exceeded by 4%. Action paused pending dual approval: Treasury + Compliance. Confidence in policy interpretation: 97%."

Lisa approves with the required co-sign from compliance. The agent logs the rationale, updates its decision memory, and continues.

What makes this powerful is how it stays current. Compliance agents continuously retrieve new rule sets from live regulatory sources, AML thresholds, sanctions updates, tax changes, through RAG-enabled sync. No more manual uploads or lagging policy documents.

When Japan tightens outbound reporting thresholds or the UK adds an entity to its sanctions list, the agent updates its logic automatically, revalidates queued transactions against the change, and issues alerts if any active case is impacted.

Every flagged decision is accompanied by a clear reasoning path:

- Sanctions Check: "Entity cross-referenced against EU Consolidated List – no match."
- AML Pattern: "No anomalous flow detected; pattern consistent with historical supplier settlement."
- Internal Policy: "Liquidity concentration exceeded threshold (limit: 20%, current: 24%). Requires joint approval."

This is visible to Lisa, her compliance officer, and auditors simultaneously, tailored views for each stakeholder. Compliance sees legal alignment. Treasury sees operational rationale. Auditors see traceable logs.

From defense to designed trust

Compliance no longer lags behind, it shapes decisions in real time. When Lisa approves that $50M transfer, she knows every rule has been checked, every threshold validated, and every rationale logged for future audit. Compliance officers no longer chase breaches after the fact; they focus on high-impact escalations with context-rich agent reports rather than sorting through false positives.

Trust isn't assumed; it's engineered. Every decision is transparent. Every action is auditable. Every agent is interruptible by design. Compliance becomes less about slowing the system down and more about making it safe enough to move faster.

Chapter 11

THE FUTURE IS AGENTIC

A gentic banking represents a transformation of institutional identity. Becoming an agentic institution means rewiring not just systems, but strategy, structure, and culture, a shift from operational execution to cognitive orchestration.

Lisa's journey reflects this transformation. Her treasury didn't just deploy agents, it redefined its operating model. Her RM teams didn't just automate tasks, they reimagined how trust is earned, how value is delivered, and how decisions are shared between human and machine.

Foundational Commitments

At the enterprise level, this shift requires foundational commitments:

- Agentic Operating Model: Every function must define what agents will do, how humans interact with and how outcomes are measured. This involves re-architecting responsibility and distributing cognition where it creates the most value.
- Technical Foundation for Intelligence: Institutions must invest in real-time data access, RAG infrastructure, LLM orchestration frameworks, and governance-as-code platforms. Without these, agents are fragile. With them, they become institutional memory in motion.
- Cultural Shift Toward Collaboration: Agents are collaborators, not competitors. Success depends on psychological safety for override and feedback, new incentives tied to agentic performance, and training for hybrid teaming.

Strategic optionality and intelligence metrics

Becoming an agentic institution means replacing control with co-creation. To fully realize agentic potential, institutions must evolve their core beliefs about value creation, control, and trust.

Lisa's organization moved from siloed functions to cross-agency collaboration frameworks. Treasury agents now coordinate with CX agents, risk models share feedback with funding optimizers, and governance systems link human oversight to machine action. This represents systemic orchestration rather than process redesign.

- Strategic Optionality: Agentic systems are modular, composable, and reconfigurable. Institutions must invest in architectures that allow them to test agents in sandboxes, swap out models as needs evolve, and experiment without breaking production. Optionality becomes a core capability.

- Metrics That Reflect Intelligence: Legacy metrics, SLAs, task completion, throughput, no longer capture the value agents deliver. Institutions must adopt new measures: time-to-outcome, proactive issue prevention, and human-agent collaboration scores. These indicators reflect institutional adaptability.

- Change Leadership at the Core: Becoming agentic requires leaders who model collaboration with agents, elevate agentic literacy across the organization, and incentivize intelligent risk-taking. Lisa isn't just a treasury head, she's a systems architect of value, guiding both humans and agents toward meaningful outcomes.

Ethical Design and Governance Evolution

Intelligence without ethics is risk. Autonomy without accountability is chaos. As institutions adopt agentic systems, ethical design becomes the foundation of trust, differentiation, and license to operate.

Lisa's institution embedded ethics into the agentic architecture itself through three principles:

- Values-Encoded Behavior: Agents were trained on institutional values, not just data. This meant preferring transparency over speed, escalating when fairness is in doubt, and avoiding optimization that sacrifices long-term trust. This represents applied value translation using prompts, policy scaffolds, and feedback loops.

- Inclusive Design Reviews: Ethical risk is contextual. Lisa's institution built multidisciplinary review boards with legal, product, tech, risk, and frontline voices. Every new agent underwent a human impact scan, asking: Who benefits? Who might be disadvantaged? What edge cases were missed? These reviews shaped better innovation rather than blocking it.

- Continuous Moral Feedback: Just as agents learn from outcomes, institutions learn from consequences. When a client feels misserved, even if compliant, the system logs it. These signals tune future behavior, machine morality in motion.

- Governance Mesh Evolution: Ethics requires execution. Lisa's institution built a governance mesh, a distributed layer of real-time checks, contextual controls, and escalation paths that guided agents like lane markers on a highway, ensuring speed with safety.

This mesh included governance-as-code infrastructure where every policy was encoded into dynamic, machine-readable modules; dual consent models requiring both system-based validation and human approval for decisions with ethical weight; and escalation as a first-class function where agents were trained to know when not to act.

Through these systems, governance becomes a co-pilot rather than a gatekeeper, accelerating action when clear, slowing it when needed, and always accountable.

Talent Strategy and Hybrid Teams

Agents may be intelligent, but institutions still run on people. In the agentic era, the workforce is reconfigured rather than replaced. Roles change, skills evolve, and mindsets must expand.

Lisa saw this transformation firsthand. Treasury specialists who once modeled cash flows now tune agent behavior. Relationship managers who used to triage client issues now co-orchestrate outcomes with digital assistants. The organization redeployed cognition rather than reducing headcount.

- Agent Fluency Across Roles: Teams must know what agents are authorized to do, how to interpret their recommendations, and when to trust, question, or override. This requires training in agentic collaboration, blending domain expertise with digital intuition.
- New Hybrid Roles: Agentic institutions create roles such as Agent Trainers (curating data, setting policy boundaries, evaluating outcomes), Ethical Stewards (reviewing agent impact, bias, and escalation), and Orchestration Analysts (designing cross-agent workflows for business value). These cross-functional hybrids are rooted in business insight and system design.
- Incentives for Collaboration: New KPIs reward agent-human synergy, reduced exception handling, and proactive insight surfacing.

Lisa's team tracks how agents improve outcomes and how humans improve agents, creating a virtuous talent loop where growth is mutual.

Institutional Learning Systems

An agentic institution develops talent continuously. In a landscape where models evolve, regulations shift, and client expectations grow, static skill sets expire quickly. What's needed is institutional learning that adapts in sync with its agents.

Lisa's organization embedded learning into every layer through operational feedback loops that refine both agent behavior and human expertise:

- Agent-Human Feedback Circuits: Every override, hesitation, or edge case flagged by a human is captured as a learning signal. These moments are reviewed by trainers, fed back into tuning cycles, and used to update prompts and scaffolds. Learning is embedded in action rather than episodic.

- Performance Heatmaps and Drift Detection: Agents are monitored for alignment with institutional goals. Dashboards show where confidence is falling, which outcomes deviate from expectation, and which agents trigger higher override rates. This allows targeted retraining and strategic resource allocation.

- Communities of Practice: Cross-functional teams meet regularly to share lessons, discuss escalations, and evolve best practices. These agentic learning collectives build institutional memory and resilience.

The institution grows with its agents, creating a workforce that is adaptive, informed, and constantly improving.

Scaling from Experiments to Ecosystems

Every institution starts its agentic journey with an experiment, but the real shift comes when that experiment scales into an ecosystem of intelligence that reshapes how the business thinks, acts, and evolves.

Lisa's organization moved through deliberate stages:

- Pilot for Precision: First agents were deployed in tightly scoped, high-impact domains, treasury forecasting, KYC document analysis, dispute resolution triage. Each was chosen for clear data availability, measurable outcomes, and low regulatory risk. The goal was credibility, not speed.

- Scale with Guardrails: Once agents proved reliable, the team expanded usage across similar contexts under strong governance with role-based access, pre-decision controls, and feedback-based tuning cycles. Teams began integrating agents across adjacent domains, liquidity optimization, RM support, and onboarding personalization.

- Institutional Integration: The tipping point came when agents became infrastructure, teammates embedded within systems rather than tools used by teams. CRM platforms surfaced agent insights, workflow engines routed based on agent triage, and governance dashboards included agent-driven actions. The institution began operating as an agentic ecosystem with intelligence distributed, outcomes coordinated, and learning continuous.

Visionary Leadership for the Agentic Era

Becoming agentic is an ongoing commitment to intelligence that evolves, systems that learn, and leadership that adapts.

Lisa's institution made this shift through mindset. The most successful agentic organizations ask not "What can we automate?" They ask, "What can we amplify, ethically, intelligently, and at scale?"

This leadership mindset includes:

- Strategic Courage: The agentic path disrupts norms, demanding the challenging of legacy roles, letting go of control in some areas, and trusting systems to reason and act. Courage here is disciplined boldness, grounded in safeguards and driven by purpose.
- Ethical Stewardship: The future is about consequence as much as capability. Leaders must take ownership of how agents make decisions, who is affected, and what values are embedded. This stewardship is a board-level, culture-wide responsibility, the heart of sustainable scale.

- Institutional Humility: No system is perfect. Every agent will encounter edge cases, bias risks, and gaps. Leading institutions learn from these publicly, transparently, and iteratively. Lisa's team adopted the mantra: "Fail small, learn fast, scale responsibly."

In the agentic era, leadership is about guiding an evolving system toward outcomes that matter, for clients, teams, and society.

Chapter 12

AI MEET BLOCKCHAIN

The Parallel Transformations

Lisa's world shows what happens when intelligence moves inside the institution. Agents perceive, reason, and act; governance becomes orchestration; decisions flow at market speed. But a second transformation is unfolding in parallel, one that reshapes the very substrate of financial services. Money and assets are becoming programmable. Tokenization, shared ledgers, and verifiable identity are no longer experiments at the edge; they are forming the new rails on which value is created, moved, and recorded.

Until now, these two revolutions have advanced on separate tracks. AI has been the language of cognition, systems understanding context and shaping intent. Blockchain has been the language of verification, systems achieving shared truth, finality, and enforceable rules without reconciliation overhead. Their convergence is not a buzzword; it is a design choice. When the agentic bank meets programmable finance, institutions gain the ability not only to decide, but to execute with embedded trust.

Think of the division of labor this way: agents translate data into intent, "rebalance liquidity now, pause this payment, adjust the hedge." Programmable rails then transform intent into enforceable state changes, transfers that settle atomically, collateral that shifts when conditions are met, and obligations that execute only when policy logic is satisfied. AI clarifies what should happen; blockchain guarantees what did happen, under precise rules. Intelligence plus trust is fused in flow.

This is not about ripping out legacy systems overnight. It is about unlocking new degrees of freedom. In treasury, tokenized deposits and cash-like instruments could allow internal sweeps and cross-border transfers to settle in seconds, complete with a cryptographic audit trail regulators can inspect in real time. In trade finance, smart contracts could release collateral when shipment data and compliance attestations align, no email chains, no midnight conference calls. In client onboarding, verifiable credentials could allow KYC agents to confirm identity proofs instantly, reducing friction without lowering standards.

For Lisa, this becomes tangible. When her liquidity agent recommends pulling surplus from one region to cover stress in another, execution today is constrained by cut-offs, correspondent schedules, and downstream reconciliation. On programmable rails, the same instruction translates into atomic transfers with embedded policy checks: limits verified, sanctions lists screened, and dual-control approvals captured on-chain, all before value moves. The reasoning remains explainable in her console; the outcome is provable on the ledger.

Convergence also reshapes accountability. In the agentic era, explainability consoles reveal why a recommendation was made. Programmable ledgers add the second layer: an immutable record of how the decision was executed, the rules invoked, the signatures applied, and the controls enforced. For boards and supervisors, this reframes the question. No longer "Do we trust the black box?" but "Can we trace the logic and verify the action?" With convergence, the answer becomes yes, on both fronts.

Boundaries still matter. Not every asset needs to be tokenized, not every workflow belongs on a chain, and not every decision should be automated end to end. The natural starting points are high-value, high-friction processes where reconciliation is costly and rule sets are clear. For low-value, high-volume flows, agentic optimization on existing rails may be more effective. The design principle is optionality: building the agentic stack to operate seamlessly across both traditional infrastructure and programmable networks, depending on economics and risk.

This chapter is not a detour into hype. It is a strategic lens on what's adjacent and inevitable. As agents become the brain of the bank, programmable finance is becoming its nervous system. One drives better decisions; the other ensures those decisions travel with integrity. In the pages ahead, we explore where this convergence is most impactful, tokenization and programmable assets, programmable money and Central bank digital currencies (CBDCs), and digital identity as a trust fabric. And we keep Lisa close, because the test for every idea remains the same: does it make an institution faster, safer, and more aligned with its purpose?

Tokenization and Programmable Assets

Lisa's institution manages trillions in liquidity, securities, and obligations. Until recently, these assets moved along familiar rails: deposits settled through correspondent banks, securities cleared by central depositories, collateral shifted only after human approval. It worked, but it was slow, costly, and fragile.

Tokenization changes that foundation. Instead of static records in siloed ledgers, assets become programmable instruments, digital representations with rules embedded directly into their design. A bond can carry not just a coupon schedule, but also eligibility constraints, collateral triggers, or settlement conditions expressed as logic. Collateral can move instantly when conditions are met, rather than waiting for reconciliation teams to confirm paperwork.

For Lisa's treasury, this shift is profound. When her liquidity agent recommends moving surplus from Frankfurt to New York, the instruction no longer queues into a batch process subject to cut-offs and correspondent schedules. On programmable rails, it executes in seconds as tokenized deposits, settling atomically across regions while simultaneously checking compliance thresholds, FX limits, and dual approvals. What was once an overnight transfer becomes a precise, conditional instruction executed with cryptographic certainty.

Programmable assets also open new levers in capital strategy. Consider structured products. In today's world, unwinding a position requires a chain of intermediaries, reconciliations, and approvals. With tokenized securities, an agent can simulate exposures and trigger a rebalancing trade in which the asset itself encodes eligibility rules and risk controls. The logic travels with the instrument, reducing disputes and accelerating execution.

Trade finance illustrates the same shift. Lisa's institution finances shipments across multiple jurisdictions. Traditionally, releasing collateral requires stacks of shipping documents, compliance attestations, and manual verification. With tokenized trade instruments, a smart contract releases funds automatically once IoT data confirms shipment arrival and compliance checks are verified on-chain. Lisa no longer convenes a war room to push paper across borders; her agents orchestrate flows that self-settle when conditions align.

Transparency is another dividend. Every programmable transfer carries an immutable record of what was executed, under what rules, and with which signatures. For supervisors and auditors, this eliminates ambiguity: it is no longer "the system says it happened," but "the ledger proves it happened."

Not every asset needs to be tokenized, and not every process benefits from programmability. But where friction is high, reconciliation is costly, and rules are clear, tokenization transforms balance sheets from static ledgers into dynamic instruments. For Lisa and her peers, this is not speculative, it is the practical foundation for agentic orchestration at institutional scale.

Programmable Money, CBDCs, Stablecoins, and Tokenized Assets

Money itself is becoming programmable. For centuries, currency has been inert, either a bearer instrument or a digital balance that moved when instructed. Central bank digital currencies (CBDCs) and tokenized deposits introduce a new paradigm: monetary instruments that carry rules, conditions, and policy levers embedded directly into their design. Alongside them, stablecoins have emerged as private-sector programmable settlement assets, already relied upon for intraday liquidity and cross-border flows. Beyond money, securities, funds, and investment products are being tokenized, embedding programmability directly into the capital markets.

For Lisa, this shift transforms both sides of her balance sheet. On the liability side, programmable money enables faster, more certain liquidity management. A funding agent can sweep balances across subsidiaries instantly, with embedded checks for sanctions, policy thresholds, or liquidity buffers. Stablecoins, running on global settlement rails, already allow corporates to move funds across borders in minutes rather than days, bypassing the frictions of correspondent banking.

On the asset side, tokenized securities unlock new tools for treasury and investment strategy. Instead of parking surplus liquidity in static overnight deposits, Lisa's agents could reallocate into tokenized money-market funds that settle and redeem instantly, with compliance and collateral verification built into the instrument. Equity or bond tokens can encode dividend distribution, voting rights, or transfer restrictions, all enforced on-chain without reconciliation delays.

This creates a new frontier: intraday liquidity optimization. Assets can be mobilized, pledged, or unwound with a speed and certainty no legacy process can match.

Consider a concrete example. Lisa's agents detect excess USD balances in New York and recommend shifting them into a tokenized short-term government bond fund. Execution is immediate: the transfer settles atomically, the fund tokens arrive in treasury's wallet, and regulators can verify the transaction in real time. If stress emerges the next morning, those same tokens can be liquidated or pledged instantly. What was once a static end-of-day process becomes a continuous liquidity lever.

The expansion into tokenized assets also blurs boundaries between treasury, trading, and investment. Agentic systems can now manage liquidity, risk, and yield as a continuous optimization problem, reallocating across cash, stablecoins, CBDCs, and tokenized securities depending on market conditions and policy rules. What matters is not the format of the asset, but its availability, liquidity, and compliance footprint, all verifiable and enforceable through blockchain rails.

But transparency and programmability also raise critical questions. Who sets the rules embedded in a tokenized fund? How do issuers guarantee resilience under stress? What safeguards prevent agents from accelerating cascades by reallocating too quickly across tokenized markets? As with programmable money, the answer lies in governance. Lisa's explainability console ensures every reallocation comes with reasoning, source validation, and a clear trace of the rules executed on-chain.

Programmability is not confined to payments; it is extending into securities, funds, and capital markets. For the agentic bank, the opportunity is to unify treasury and investment under a single cognitive and operational fabric, where liquidity and risk move fluidly across both money and assets. The challenge is to ensure that programmability does not outpace prudence.

Digital Identity and Verifiable Credentials

If programmable money defines how value moves, digital identity defines who can participate. For Lisa's institution, every decision, whether processing a payment, extending credit, or executing a trade, rests on trust in the counterparty's identity. In the agentic era, this trust cannot be slow or manual. It must be embedded, verifiable, and machine-readable.

Digital identity frameworks and verifiable credentials make this possible. Powered by blockchain and decentralized standards, they establish trust primitives: tamper-proof attestations of who an individual, institution, or asset is. Instead of repeatedly asking clients for documents, institutions can rely on credentials issued by trusted authorities, regulators, employers, or banks, that Lisa's agents can verify instantly.

Consider onboarding. When her compliance agent encounters a new counterparty, it doesn't trigger a week-long KYC review. Instead, it queries a digital credential cryptographically signed by a trusted registry, confirming both identity and regulatory standing. Within seconds, the agent verifies it, checks embedded conditions, permitted jurisdictions, transaction limits, and greenlights the trade within policy. Fraud risk is reduced, compliance is satisfied, and the client experiences speed without sacrificing rigor.

The implications extend beyond onboarding. Imagine a regulator issuing a sanctions update. In legacy systems, it might take days for all institutions to refresh databases, leaving gaps in enforcement. With verifiable credentials, an update can instantly revoke access for sanctioned entities across the ecosystem. Lisa's compliance agent receives the new credential in real time and automatically adjusts its rules, no manual intervention required.

Digital identity also enhances personalization. Lisa's client intelligence agents can tailor recommendations not just from transaction history, but from verified attributes such as corporate structure, credit rating, sustainability certifications, or ESG disclosures. Each credential is cryptographically secure and auditable, ensuring personalization rests on authentic data, not assumptions.

Risks remain. Over-centralized identity systems risk surveillance overreach; over-fragmented ones risk inefficiency and inconsistency. The solution is balance: distributed identity frameworks with clear governance, interoperability standards, and safeguards for selective disclosure. Lisa's agents only need what is relevant, verifying that a client meets regulatory thresholds, not exposing their entire history.

In practice, digital identity turns compliance from a burden into an enabler. Instead of slowing transactions, it accelerates them. Instead of adding friction, it builds trust into the rails. For the agentic bank, identity is not paperwork; it is a living trust fabric that agents can access, interpret, and enforce in real time.

Where AI and Blockchain Converge

AI interprets and decides. Blockchain verifies and enforces. When these two forces converge, institutions gain both intelligence and trust, fused into a single operating fabric.

For Lisa, the value is immediate. Her agents can recommend reallocating liquidity, approving credit, or executing a hedge. But execution is where intent meets risk. Blockchain rails provide programmable certainty: every action is tied to predefined policy rules, enforced cryptographically, and recorded immutably. The reasoning trail she sees in her explainability console is mirrored by a verifiable transaction trail on the ledger. Thought and action align in one continuous loop.

Consider liquidity management. Lisa's treasury agent detects a $50M funding shortfall and recommends shifting balances from Frankfurt to New York. On legacy rails, execution involves cut-off times, intermediaries, and reconciliation delays. On programmable rails, the same instruction triggers an atomic transfer of tokenized deposits, complete with sanctions checks, policy limits, and dual approvals. AI clarifies what should happen; blockchain guarantees how it happened, and proves it, step by step.

The same holds in client service. Lisa's client co-pilot may generate a restructuring proposal. Once accepted, a smart contract adjusts collateral positions, sweeps balances, and updates regulatory filings in one flow. Intelligence sits in the agent; enforceability sits in the contract. Clients experience seamless service, regulators gain transparency, and the institution reduces operational drag.

This convergence also unlocks systemic trust. Real-time regulatory reporting, once a costly, after-the-fact process, can be delivered directly through shared ledgers, with agents curating the insights supervisors most need. Cross-institutional collaboration, such as syndicated loans or shared KYC utilities, becomes simpler when agents negotiate and blockchains record, ensuring both adaptability and accountability. Even client contracts evolve from static PDFs into living instruments, executing themselves while agents interpret context and manage exceptions.

Yet convergence raises systemic stakes. Agents acting on blockchain rails can accelerate liquidity cascades if not governed properly. Smart contracts can bind institutions into unintended commitments if conditions are poorly designed. Transparency can improve oversight, but also expose competitive information. These risks are not reasons to avoid convergence; they are reasons to design it deliberately, with governance meshes and trust scaffolds that balance efficiency with prudence.

The bigger picture is clear: AI makes decisions intelligent; blockchain makes them trustworthy. Together, they redefine what it means for an institution to act with both speed and integrity. For the agentic bank, convergence is not hype, it is the architecture of systems where intelligence does not outpace trust, and where trust does not slow down intelligence.

The Convergence Playbook: How to Prepare for AI + Blockchain

For leaders, convergence is not a technology experiment, it is a design choice. Preparing for it requires intention, discipline, and early alignment across strategy, operations, and governance. A practical playbook includes five moves:

1. Identify High-Friction Use Cases

Start where today's systems create the most drag. Cross-border liquidity transfers that take days, trade finance workflows bound by manual document checks, or KYC refresh cycles that stall onboarding are prime candidates. These are not speculative pilots; they are pain points with measurable ROI if solved.

2. Pilot Dual Integration

Don't run blockchain pilots in isolation, and don't let agents remain disconnected from execution rails. Pair them. For example, deploy a liquidity agent in advisory mode while simultaneously testing programmable deposits or tokenized cash instruments for settlement. The agent recommends; the programmable rail executes. Both are monitored through explainability consoles and on-chain audit trails.

3. Embed Governance Early

Programmable assets raise regulatory questions, and agents raise explainability concerns. Address both at once by codifying policy-as-code (using tools like OPA or Sentinel) and requiring every programmable transaction to carry:

- A reasoning trail (why the agent recommended it).
- A verification trail (how the programmable rail executed it).

This dual logging creates audit-ready workflows regulators can trust.

4. Design for Interoperability

Avoid locking into a single blockchain or protocol. Use modular orchestration layers so agents can transact across legacy rails, private blockchains, or public tokenized markets as needed. The goal is optionality, future-proofing so that strategy is not constrained by premature bets on one infrastructure.

5. Build Fusion Teams for Convergence

Convergence cannot be siloed in IT or treasury. Create fusion pods that blend treasury, risk, compliance, and technology leaders. Their mandate:

run pilots that prove end-to-end flows (decision →
execution → audit) and define guardrails for scale.
New roles will emerge, such as Agentic-Blockchain
Stewards, leaders responsible for ensuring that
when intelligence meets programmability, institutional values and controls remain intact.

A Practical Playbook for Convergence, Lisa's Lens

Convergence becomes real only when seen in practice. Lisa's institution approached it step by step,
targeting friction points and proving value before
scaling.

1. Identify High-Friction Use Cases

Lisa's treasury team began by mapping pain points.
Cross-border liquidity transfers often took 24–48
hours due to settlement lags and manual compliance checks. Syndicated loan servicing created
reconciliation headaches across multiple banks.
KYC refreshes stalled high-value client onboarding.
These weren't minor inefficiencies, they were costs
measured in millions. Lisa's first move wasn't to
tokenize everything. It was to pinpoint the workflows where programmable assets plus intelligent
agents could deliver undeniable value.

2. Pilot Dual Integration

The first pilot combined her liquidity agent with tokenized deposits issued on a permissioned blockchain. At 10:00 a.m., the liquidity agent detected tightening buffers in Singapore. Instead of waiting on cut-off times, it proposed reallocating €25M of surplus from Frankfurt. Execution ran through programmable deposits: the agent instructed the move while the blockchain rail verified pre-coded conditions, sanctions screening, dual authorization, and liquidity thresholds. Settlement completed in under 30 seconds, with both reasoning (from the agent) and proof-of-execution (from the ledger) logged in Lisa's console. This was convergence in motion: AI narrating the why, blockchain enforcing the how.

3. Embed Governance Early

Every pilot transaction carried two parallel logs:
- A reasoning trail: "Reallocation justified by forecast shortfall of €18M under stress scenario. Confidence: 91%."
- A verification trail: "Executed via Tokenized Deposit Rail v2.1. Compliance check: Basel liquidity thresholds confirmed. Approval: dual sign-off recorded."

Lisa's compliance officer could view both in a single console. Regulators were given access to the verification trail through an immutable audit dashboard. Governance wasn't bolted on later, it was woven into the pilot from the first test.

4. Design for Interoperability

Lisa's agents were not confined to blockchain-only workflows. On Monday, a liquidity transfer used programmable deposits. On Tuesday, a client sweep relied on Fedwire. On Wednesday, a high-value FX settlement used a private consortium ledger. Her orchestration layer allowed agents to select the right rail based on timing, cost, and policy. Interoperability gave her optionality, proof that convergence was not a bet-the-bank leap, but a controlled expansion of capabilities.

5. Build Fusion Teams for Convergence

Lisa did not leave convergence to IT or treasury alone. Her fusion pod included treasury operators, blockchain engineers, compliance leads, and risk officers. A new role emerged: the Agentic-Blockchain Steward, responsible for monitoring how AI and programmable rails interacted. When Lisa overrode a recommendation, the steward ensured the reasoning loop updated. When a blockchain rail flagged a policy conflict, the steward coordinated fixes. Governance became not a committee, but a living function embedded in daily operations.

Lisa's Tokenized Fund Scenario: Investing Through Convergence

By mid-afternoon, Lisa shifts from liquidity to her institution's investment portfolio. A major client wants exposure to a new tokenized bond fund, an ETF-equivalent issued on a regulated blockchain network, where each unit is a programmable token representing fractionalized bond holdings.

Her investment strategy agent runs the first pass. It ingests macro conditions, credit spreads, and FX exposure. The reasoning trail is clear: "Client allocation to fixed income is 6% below policy target. Tokenized bond fund offers higher liquidity efficiency via instant settlement. Confidence: 87%." Lisa reviews the recommendation and gives a provisional green light.

Here's how convergence plays out:

- AI interprets and recommends. The agent generates the investment rationale.
- Blockchain executes. Tokens transfer instantly into the client's wallet, with AML, KYC, and suitability checks validated on-chain.
- Governance embeds itself. The compliance mesh automatically attaches policy references, jurisdictional caps, and ESG alignment tags.

For the client, the experience is transformative. Instead of waiting two business days for trade settlement, reconciliation, and custodian confirmation, holdings update within seconds. Alongside the portfolio shift, the client sees a transparent reasoning log: "Allocation adjusted to improve liquidity profile; fund tokens verified against sustainability criteria."

Lisa's role is not to push paper but to validate alignment. Her override option remains active; she can reject the trade if macro conditions shift or if the client's appetite changes. Every action, recommendation, override, and execution is captured as traceable, explainable, and verifiable.

Lisa's Stablecoin Settlement Scenario: Cross-Border Payments at Machine Speed

Late in the day, Lisa faces a client escalation. A corporate customer needs to settle an urgent supplier payment from New York to Singapore. On traditional rails, cut-off times mean funds wouldn't clear until the following business day, creating both reputational and contractual risk.

Her FX and payments agent surfaces the issue instantly:

- Reasoning trail: "Settlement request exceeds time window on SWIFT/Fedwire rails. Alternative available: settle via regulated USD stablecoin (USDC) issued by a bank consortium, with on-chain compliance checks. Confidence: 92%."

- Policy context: "Permitted under cross-border pilot program, subject to daily volume thresholds and AML/KYC on both ends."

Lisa reviews the options in her explainability console:
1. Traditional settlement, delayed, but guaranteed by legacy rails.
2. Stablecoin settlement, instant, with tokenized transfer finality in seconds.

She approves option two. Execution unfolds seamlessly:
- The agent initiates the stablecoin transfer from the client's USDC balance to the supplier's wallet.
- Embedded smart contracts verify both counterparties against sanctions and KYC registries.
- The blockchain network provides real-time settlement finality and an immutable audit trail.
- The compliance mesh auto-generates a regulatory reporting packet: "Cross-border payment, $12.5M equivalent, settled via stablecoin, policy ref. 2025-TRX-04."

For the client, funds arrive instantly. For Lisa's institution, the transaction is faster, cheaper, and fully compliant. The agent logs its reasoning, "settlement urgency + stablecoin channel available + within limits", while the blockchain ledger proves execution integrity.

Lisa reflects: a year ago, this would have triggered a late-night escalation, with lawyers, operations, and risk officers debating options. Now, intelligence and trust rails converge. The AI agent interprets context, the stablecoin rail executes securely, and governance ensures nothing slips through.

Strategic Questions for Leaders

For leaders, the convergence of AI and blockchain is not simply a technology choice, it is a design choice for the future of their institutions. The question is not if these systems will meet, but how deliberately they will be brought together. The institutions that thrive will be those that shape convergence with foresight rather than stumble into it by accident.

Several questions frame the leadership agenda:

- How do we design for interoperability?

   Agentic systems must operate seamlessly across traditional rails, tokenized assets, and programmable money. Committing too early to a single standard or network risks limiting flexibility. The strategic path is optionality, ensuring agents can transact across both old and new infrastructures as economics and regulation dictate.

- What boundaries should be set?

  Not every process belongs on-chain, and not every decision should be automated end-to-end. Leaders must distinguish between workflows where programmability adds resilience and those where human discretion remains paramount.

- How do we balance efficiency with systemic risk?

  Agents executing instantly on tokenized markets may remove friction but also amplify shocks. Liquidity cascades, flash defaults, or regulatory blind spots can be triggered by the same speed that makes programmable finance attractive. Guardrails are not afterthoughts, they are the architecture of safety.

- What role do regulators play?

  Shared ledgers and programmable money make real-time supervision possible. Institutions must lean into this opportunity: engaging supervisors early, codifying explainability standards, and designing systems that are auditable by default rather than patched after deployment.

- What will stewardship look like in convergence?

  Yesterday's leaders were stewards of capital. Tomorrow's must be stewards of intelligence and trust. The responsibility is not only to scale technology, but to encode values, fairness, transparency, resilience, into the systems that now carry financial life.

Closing Perspective

For Lisa, convergence is not abstract. It is the difference between a treasury decision that remains a recommendation and one that settles instantly with integrity. It is the difference between compliance as a manual review and compliance as a living credential verified in real time. It is the difference between clients waiting for fragmented updates and clients experiencing services that feel seamless, personalized, and trustworthy.

If agentic intelligence is becoming the brain of the bank, then blockchain and programmable finance are becoming its nervous system. One interprets and decides; the other verifies and enforces. Together, they allow institutions not only to think and act, but to transact, record, and govern with unprecedented speed and certainty.

The challenge for leaders is to shape this convergence with clarity, ensuring that intelligence and trust advance hand in hand. The future of banking will not be written in AI alone or blockchain alone, but in the way they are brought together.

The institutions that seize this moment will not simply run faster. They will operate on a new plane, where judgment, execution, and trust move as one.

chapter 13

THE AGENTIC TREASURY: IMPLEMENTATION GUIDE

Companion Video: Lisa and her AI Agents

Before you proceed with this section, scan the QR code below to watch the video.

The companion video introduces Lisa, the corporate treasurer of a multinational enterprise operating across Latin America. Her mandate is clear: safeguard liquidity, optimize cash positioning, enforce compliance, and mitigate financial risk in an increasingly volatile world.

Treasury has always been a function of precision. But precision alone is no longer enough. Today, volatility moves faster than reporting cycles. Liquidity risks emerge between closing reports. Market signals shift before committees can convene. The gap between analysis and action has become a source of exposure.

In the video, Lisa does not confront this complexity alone.

She works alongside three AI Treasury Agents, each embedded within the Treasury Platform and governed by institutional controls:

Maria — Forecasting & Risk Analyst

Maria generates predictive cash flow models, runs scenario simulations, and identifies liquidity gaps weeks in advance. She applies advanced analytics to detect anomalies, highlight vulnerabilities, and flag early warning signals before exposure materializes. Unlike traditional forecasting tools that rely on historical patterns, Maria continuously learns from emerging market conditions and internal cash behavior.

Alejandro — Liquidity & Investment Analyst

Alejandro evaluates funding strategies across credit facilities, intercompany transfers, and idle subsidiary balances. He simulates trade-offs between cost, timing, and risk, always operating within treasury policy constraints. When Maria identifies a shortfall, Alejandro immediately models optimal responses, whether through cash reallocation, credit facility draws, or payment timing adjustments.

Sam — Transaction & Operations Analyst

Sam tracks inbound and outbound payments in real time across multiple payment networks. He reconciles expected flows against actual settlement data, monitors exceptions, and provides confirmation with precise timing and full audit visibility. Sam eliminates the uncertainty that often delays treasury decisions: "Has the payment arrived? Can we proceed?"

Together, they illustrate a structural shift in treasury:
- Reactive becomes predictive
- Manual becomes automated
- Transactional becomes strategic

But the video is not about digital assistants responding to prompts. It is about infrastructure.

Beyond Agents: The Orchestration Layer

What makes the system institutional-grade is not the agents themselves. It is the orchestration layer that governs them.

Individual AI agents, however sophisticated, cannot deliver enterprise treasury capability. They become powerful only when coordinated through a control plane that enforces policy, sequences workflows, and maintains human authority.

This orchestration layer ensures:
- ERP systems, Treasury Management Systems, and bank APIs operate in coordination
- Forecasting, liquidity optimization, and transaction monitoring are synchronized
- Policies, thresholds, and approval requirements are automatically enforced
- Every recommendation is traceable, auditable, and subject to human authority

Without orchestration, agents are tools. With orchestration, they become part of a controlled operating model.

Purpose of This Field Guide

The video demonstrates what human–AI collaboration in treasury looks like. This technical field guide explains how it works and how to build it safely.

Over the following pages, we will:

- Deconstruct the system architecture and explain why each layer matters
- Explain the orchestration control plane and its governance mechanisms
- Detail Agentic RAG and how grounded intelligence differs from generic AI
- Walk through forecasting, liquidity optimization, and transaction monitoring workflows
- Define governance, auditability, and explainability requirements for regulated environments
- Outline deployment considerations and phased implementation strategies for enterprise treasury

This is not a conceptual exercise. It is a deployable model built on production treasury infrastructure.

What follows is both a technical specification and an architectural philosophy. You will see detailed workflows, implementation tables, and system blueprints. But more importantly, you will see a set of principles: governance before intelligence, evidence over patterns, transparency by design, human authority preserved. These principles determine whether AI becomes an institutional asset or an institutional risk. The choice of how to build matters as much as the decision to build at all.

1. The Architectural Anchor: The Deployable Agentic Treasury Architecture

From Human Authority to Governed Execution

The Agentic Treasury Platform is not an AI overlay added to treasury operations. It is a structured, policy-governed architecture that embeds intelligence into institutional infrastructure.

Unlike chatbot interfaces or standalone AI tools, this architecture integrates human authority, orchestration logic, agent intelligence, data grounding, and financial execution into a cohesive system. Each layer serves a distinct purpose. Together, they create a treasury operating model that is both intelligent and institutionally controlled.

The model below illustrates how these components work as one system.

Architectural Layers & Responsibilities

1. Human Authority Layer

The treasury professional remains the decision-maker and approval authority. The interface provides natural language interaction, real-time dashboards, and authorization controls. AI recommendations are presented here—never executed autonomously.

Technical Blueprint: Agentic Treasury Stack

HUMAN AUTHORITY LAYER

Lisa – Corporate Treasurer
- Decision-maker
- Approval authority

Treasury Platform UI (Web/Voice Interface)
- Dashboards
- Natural language interaction
- Authorization controls

ORCHESTRATION LAYER (Institutional Control Plane)
- Workflow engine
- Agent routing
- Policy enforcement
- Approval checkpoints
- Audit logging
- Cross-agent coordination

AGENT INTELLIGENCE LAYER

Maria — Forecasting & Risk
Alejandro — Liquidity Optimization
Sam — Transaction Monitoring

Powered by:
- Agentic RAG
- Large Language Models (GPT, Claude, Gemini)
- Structured decision logic

DATA & KNOWLEDGE LAYER

Internal Sources:
- ERP Systems (SAP, Oracle)
- Treasury Management Systems (Kyriba, FIS, Reval)
- Data Warehouse (Snowflake, BigQuery)
- Internal Treasury Policies

External Sources:
- Market Data APIs (Rates, FX, Macro Signals)
- Payment Networks (SWIFT, FedNow, SEPA)
- Compliance & Sanctions Databases

EXECUTION & GOVERNANCE LAYER
- Payment gateways
- Bank APIs
- Credit facilities
- Regulatory reporting
- Audit trail & explainability console
  All high-value actions require human authorization.

2. Orchestration Layer
(Institutional Control Plane)

This is the governance backbone. It routes requests to appropriate agents, enforces treasury policies, coordinates multi-agent workflows, inserts approval checkpoints, and maintains comprehensive audit logs. Without this layer, agents operate in isolation. With it, they operate as a controlled system.

3. Agent Intelligence Layer

Specialized AI agents—Maria, Alejandro, and Sam—provide domain-specific intelligence. They leverage Agentic RAG to ground recommendations in real data, apply large language models for reasoning, and execute structured decision logic. Each agent has a defined scope and operates within policy boundaries set by orchestration.

4. Data & Knowledge Layer

Intelligence requires accurate, timely data. This layer integrates internal systems (ERP, TMS, data warehouses, policy repositories) with external sources (market data, payment networks, compliance databases). Data is retrieved on-demand, versioned for auditability, and validated before use.

5. Execution & Governance Layer

Once authorized by a human, actions are executed through payment gateways, bank APIs, and credit facilities. Regulatory reporting occurs automatically. Every action generates an immutable audit trail accessible through the explainability console. High-value transactions require explicit human authorization—never just policy compliance.

Architectural Principle

The system is **governance-first, intelligence-- enabled**.
- The human remains accountable
- The orchestration layer controls decisions
- AI agents provide grounded recommendations
- Data ensures accuracy
- Execution remains policy-bound

This is what makes the architecture deployable in regulated financial environments.

This architecture is the backbone upon which all subsequent sections are built. Each component depends on the others. Remove orchestration, and governance collapses. Remove data grounding, and recommendations become unreliable. Remove human authority, and institutional accountability disappears.

The system is designed to fail safely: when uncertainty arises, control escalates to humans.

Key Content Enhancements:

1. **Added contrasting statement**: "Unlike chatbot interfaces or standalone AI tools..." — clarifies what this architecture is NOT
2. **Enhanced layer descriptions**: Each of the 5 layers now has a dedicated paragraph explaining its purpose and importance
3. **Strengthened interconnection narrative**: Added final paragraph explaining dependencies between layers and fail-safe design
4. **Improved architectural principle section**: Reformatted for better visual hierarchy and added emphasis
5. **Added practical context**: Included explanation of why each layer matters to the overall system integrity
6. **Clearer differentiation**: Made explicit that "policy compliance ≠ human authorization" for high-value transactions
7. **Better transitions**: Added connecting phrases to show how sections relate to each other

The section now provides both the technical blueprint AND the conceptual framework for understanding why the architecture is designed this way.

2. The Orchestration Layer: The Institutional Control Plane

Why Orchestration Comes First

In the video, Lisa appears to interact directly with Maria, Alejandro, and Sam.

In reality, she does not.

Every request flows through a dedicated orchestration layer that coordinates intelligence, enforces policy, and maintains institutional control. This layer is invisible to the user but essential to the system's integrity.

Without orchestration:
- Agents operate independently
- Governance becomes fragmented
- Auditability breaks down
- Risk increases

With orchestration:
- Intelligence becomes structured
- Decisions become traceable
- Human authority remains intact

The orchestration layer is not an enhancement. It is the operating system of the Agentic Treasury.

The Core Responsibilities of Orchestration

The orchestration layer performs five core functions that transform isolated AI agents into a coordinated treasury intelligence system.

1. Intent Routing

When Lisa asks a question, the orchestration layer determines:
- Which agent should respond
- Which data sources are required
- Whether approvals may be needed later
- What context from previous interactions is relevant

Example:
- "Show me next quarter's cash forecast" → Maria
- "How should we cover this shortfall?" → Alejandro
- "Has the Brazil payment arrived?" → Sam
- "What's our current liquidity position across all entities?" → Maria + Sam (coordinated)

The routing logic is not hardcoded—it adapts based on the treasury's current state, pending workflows, and policy requirements.

2. Workflow Coordination

Treasury decisions rarely involve one agent. Complex questions require collaboration.
  The orchestration layer:
- Sequences agent interactions
- Combines outputs into coherent recommendations
- Resolves conflicts between agent recommendations
- Maintains conversation context across multi-turn workflows

Example: When Alejandro recommends drawing a credit facility to address a shortfall, orchestration automatically:
1. Checks Maria's risk assessment for conflicting signals
2. Verifies current facility utilization against policy limits
3. Queries Sam for pending settlements that might reduce the need
4. Presents a unified recommendation only after all checks pass

This coordination happens in milliseconds, invisible to Lisa.

3. Policy Enforcement

Before any recommendation reaches Lisa, policies are applied automatically:
- Liquidity buffer thresholds
- Exposure limits by counterparty and geography
- Approval hierarchies based on transaction size
- Compliance rules (sanctions screening, regulatory constraints)
- Operational controls (settlement cutoff times, trading hours)

Policy is enforced as code, not manual review. Non-compliant options are filtered out before Lisa ever sees them.

Example: If Alejandro identifies that delaying a supplier payment would violate the company's 60-day DPO policy, that option is automatically removed from the recommendation set—even if it's financially optimal.

4. Human-in-the-Loop Control

The orchestration layer inserts mandatory approvals at critical decision points:
- High-value payments (above defined thresholds)
- Credit facility usage

- Risk escalations
- Policy exceptions or overrides
- New counterparty transactions

This ensures AI informs decisions but never overrides institutional authority. The approval gates are configurable based on role, transaction type, and risk level.

Example: When Sam confirms a payment has settled and Alejandro recommends executing a $5M supplier payment, orchestration triggers an approval workflow because the amount exceeds the treasurer's authorization limit. The CFO receives a notification with full context and explainability before execution proceeds.

5. Audit and Explainability

Every orchestration event is logged with complete traceability:
- Inputs used (user query, system state)
- Data sources accessed (with timestamps)
- Agents invoked (and their response times)
- Policies applied (and which passed/failed)
- Human approvals recorded (who, when, decision)
- Execution outcomes

These records feed the Explainability Console discussed in Section 8. They also support regulatory audits, internal compliance reviews, and model governance requirements.

The audit trail is immutable and cryptographically signed to ensure integrity.

Technical Blueprint — Orchestration Workflow

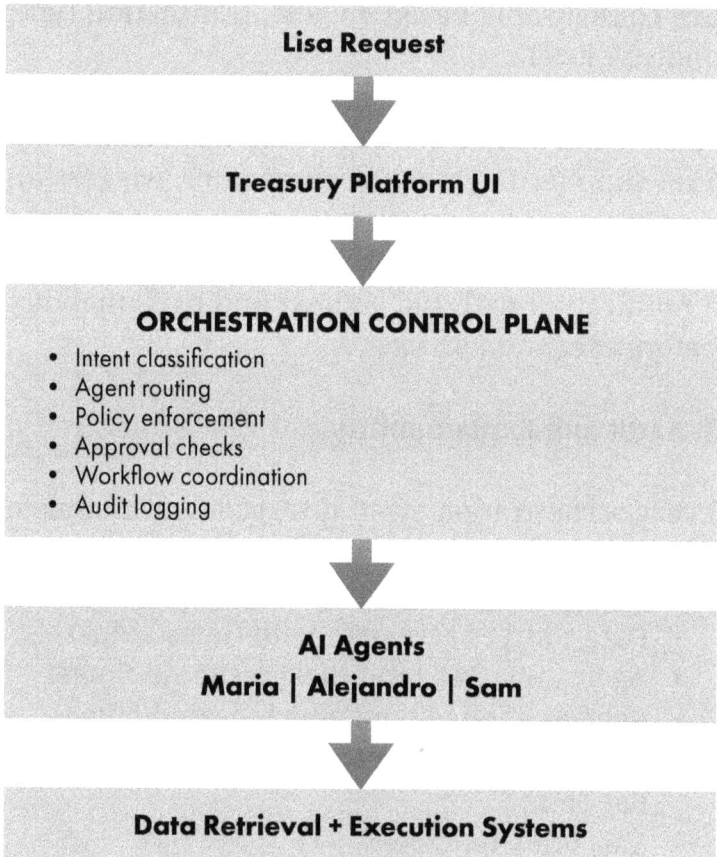

Lisa Request

⬇

Treasury Platform UI

⬇

ORCHESTRATION CONTROL PLANE
- Intent classification
- Agent routing
- Policy enforcement
- Approval checks
- Workflow coordination
- Audit logging

⬇

AI Agents
Maria | Alejandro | Sam

⬇

Data Retrieval + Execution Systems

Implementation Table — Building the Orchestration Layer

Function	Purpose	Example Technologies	Implementation Notes
Work-flow Engine	Coordinate multi-step processes	Temporal, Camunda, AWS Step Functions	Stateless services recommended; supports retries and rollbacks
Agent Router	Direct requests to correct agent(s)	LangGraph, LangChain, custom orchestrator	Driven by intent classification; supports multi-agent coordination
Policy Engine	Enforce treasury rules	Open Policy Agent, custom rules engine	Externalized policy configs; version-controlled
Approval System	Human authorization checkpoints	IAM + Treasury UI integration	Role-based access control; mobile-enabled for urgent approvals
Audit Logging	Full traceability	Splunk, Data-dog, ELK stack, CloudWatch	Immutable logs; WORM storage recommended

Implementation Guidance (Practical)

Most institutions do not build this all at once.
Recommended rollout:

1. **Deploy orchestration layer with logging first** — Establish the control plane before adding intelligence

2. **Integrate one treasury workflow (forecasting)** — Prove governance model with lowest-risk use case
3. **Add policy enforcement** — Codify existing treasury policies before expanding scope
4. **Introduce additional agents progressively** — Add Alejandro, then Sam, after Maria is stable
5. **Expand automation only after governance is stable** — Speed follows control, not vice versa

This sequence minimizes operational risk and builds institutional confidence incrementally.

Critical implementation principle: The orchestration layer must be production-ready before the first agent goes live. Retrofitting governance after deployment creates technical debt and operational risk.

Key Principle

The orchestration layer ensures that:
- AI agents collaborate safely within defined boundaries
- Data is used responsibly and traceably
- Humans remain accountable for all consequential decisions

It transforms isolated intelligence into institutional capability.

Without orchestration, you have AI tools. With orchestration, you have an intelligent treasury operating model.

3. Agentic RAG: How Intelligence Is Grounded in Treasury Data

Why Language Models Alone Are Not Enough

Large Language Models are powerful reasoning tools, but by themselves they present two critical problems for institutional treasury environments:
- They rely on training memory, which may be outdated or incomplete
- They may generate plausible-sounding responses without verifiable source grounding

In treasury, this is unacceptable.
Decisions must be:
- **Current** — Reflecting real-time market conditions and cash positions
- **Evidence-based** — Grounded in actual enterprise data, not statistical patterns
- **Traceable** — Auditable back to specific source systems and data points
- **Policy-aware** — Constrained by institutional rules and regulatory requirements

This is why Maria and the other AI agents operate using **Agentic Retrieval-Augmented Generation (Agentic RAG).**

What Agentic RAG Means in Practice

Traditional RAG works as follows:
1. Retrieve documents based on keyword or semantic similarity
2. Attach them to a prompt as context
3. Generate a response from the combined input

This approach is passive. The retrieval happens once, at the beginning, and doesn't adapt based on what the model discovers.

Agentic RAG adds a higher layer of intelligence.

The agent actively decides:
- What information is required to answer the query
- Which specific data sources should be queried (and in what order)
- Whether retrieved data is sufficient or if additional context is needed
- If clarification from the user or escalation to another agent is required
- How to handle conflicting information across sources

In other words: **Retrieval is dynamic, contextual, and policy-aware.**

The agent can make multiple retrieval calls, refine its queries based on intermediate findings, and validate information against policy constraints before formulating a response.

Example — Lisa Requests a Forecast

When Lisa asks: *"Maria, show me our projected cash flow for the next 90 days."*

Maria does not immediately answer. She doesn't have the information in memory.

Behind the scenes, Agentic RAG executes the following workflow:

1. Intent Classification

Orchestration identifies this as a forecasting request and routes to Maria.

2. Data Planning

Maria determines required sources:
- ERP systems — Accounts payable/receivable schedules
- TMS — Current cash positions across all entities

- Data warehouse — Historical payment patterns and seasonal trends
- Market data feeds — FX rates, interest rate projections
- Policy repository — Minimum liquidity buffer requirements

3. Retrieval Orchestration

Maria queries each system:
- Pulls upcoming obligations from ERP (next 90 days)
- Retrieves current balances from TMS
- Analyzes payment timing patterns from historical data
- Fetches latest FX forecasts for multi-currency exposure
- Loads applicable treasury policies

4. Context Assembly

Retrieved data is structured into a coherent context, normalized for cross-system consistency, and time-aligned for the 90-day horizon.

5. LLM Reasoning

Maria's foundation model analyzes the complete context to:
- Project daily cash positions

- Identify expected inflows and outflows
- Calculate net positions by week
- Account for currency translation effects

6. Risk Evaluation

The model scans for:
- Projected liquidity shortfalls
- Policy buffer violations
- Concentration risks by entity or currency
- Timing mismatches between inflows and obligations

7. Response Generation

Maria delivers a structured forecast with:
- Visual cash flow projection
- Narrative explanation of key drivers
- Flagged risk periods (e.g., "Week 7 shows a potential $4.2M shortfall")
- Recommended actions if thresholds are breached

If Maria identifies a significant liquidity gap, orchestration automatically notifies Alejandro to begin evaluating funding options—before Lisa even asks.

Agentic RAG Architecture (Technical Blueprint)

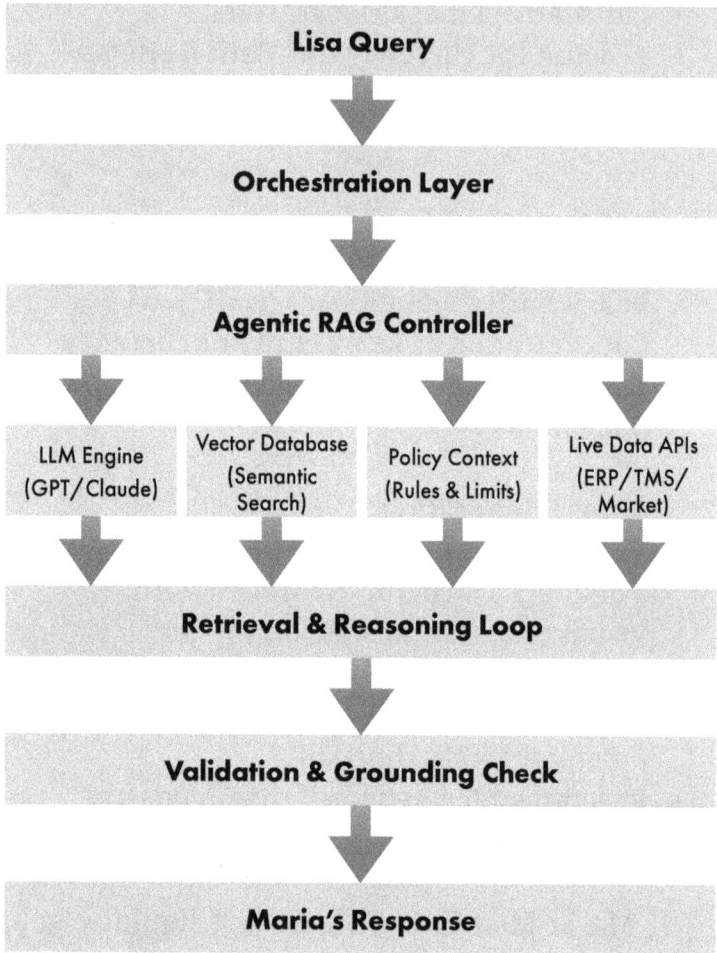

Lisa Query

↓

Orchestration Layer

↓

Agentic RAG Controller

↓

| LLM Engine (GPT/Claude) | Vector Database (Semantic Search) | Policy Context (Rules & Limits) | Live Data APIs (ERP/TMS/Market) |

↓

Retrieval & Reasoning Loop

↓

Validation & Grounding Check

↓

Maria's Response

Data Sources Used by Agentic RAG

Internal Enterprise Data:
- ERP systems (SAP, Oracle) — Payables, receivables, purchase orders
- Treasury Management Systems (Kyriba, FIS, Reval) — Cash positions, hedging, investments
- Data warehouse (Snowflake, BigQuery) — Historical transaction patterns, analytics
- Document repositories — Treasury policies, approval matrices, counterparty agreements
- Identity & access systems — Authorization hierarchies, role definitions

External Data:
- Market data providers (Bloomberg, Refinitiv) — FX rates, interest rates, commodity prices
- Payment networks (SWIFT, FedNow) — Settlement status, network conditions
- Regulatory databases — Sanctions lists, compliance requirements, reporting standards
- Credit rating agencies — Counterparty risk data, sovereign risk assessments
- Economic indicators — Central bank policies, macro forecasts, geopolitical risk signals

The LLM never guesses. It reasons over retrieved evidence. Every statement in Maria's response can be traced back to a specific data source with a timestamp.

Implementation Table — Agentic RAG Components

Component	Function	Example Technologies	Implementation Notes
Foundation LLM	Reasoning & synthesis	GPT-4, Claude Sonnet, Gemini	Multiple models may coexist; selection based on task requirements
Vector Database	Semantic retrieval	Pinecone, Weaviate, FAISS, Chroma	Stores embedded enterprise knowledge; updated nightly or real-time
Retrieval Engine	Data selection logic	LangChain, LlamaIndex, custom retrievers	Must support policy-aware filtering and multi-source federation
Data Connectors	System integration	REST APIs, gRPC, ETL pipelines	Real-time where possible; cached with TTL for performance
Policy Context Engine	Governance constraints	Open Policy Agent, custom rules	Enforces treasury rules during retrieval and reasoning
Validation Layer	Grounding verification	Custom logic, fact-checking modules	Prevents hallucinations; flags low-confidence responses

Why This Matters

Agentic RAG prevents two common AI failures in enterprise environments:

✗ **Hallucinated insights** — Confident-sounding answers based on no actual data

✗ **Stale or unverified recommendations** — Decisions based on outdated or incorrect information

Instead, it produces:

✓ **Evidence-grounded reasoning** — Every recommendation traces to real data

✓ **Institutionally compliant outputs** — Policy constraints applied during generation

✓ **Traceable decision logic** — Full audit trail of sources and reasoning steps

✓ **Adaptive intelligence** — Retrieval adjusts based on what the model learns during reasoning
This is what allows Maria to function as a trusted forecasting partner rather than a chatbot.

The Difference in Practice

Traditional LLM	Agentic RAG
"Based on typical patterns, you might see a shortfall around mid-quarter."	"Week 7 shows a projected $4.2M shortfall based on: $8.5M payables due (ERP-2024-02-14), $3.1M expected inflows (TMS-Entity-BR), and minimum buffer requirement of $2M (Policy-LATAM-001)."
Plausible	Verifiable

Key Principle

Agentic RAG does not make decisions.

It ensures that when humans make decisions, they do so with:

- **Complete context** — All relevant information surfaced automatically
- **Relevant evidence** — Data selected intelligently, not just retrieved broadly
- **Policy-aware intelligence** — Recommendations that respect institutional constraints from the start

This transforms AI from a liability into an institutional asset.

4. Alejandro: Liquidity Optimization as an Agentic Workflow

From Forecast to Action

Maria's role is to understand what might happen.

Alejandro's role is to determine what should be done about it.

When Maria identifies a projected liquidity shortfall, the system does not automatically execute a solution. Instead, the orchestration layer activates Alejandro to evaluate funding options within institutional constraints.

This transforms treasury decision-making from reactive analysis into proactive optimization.

The Liquidity Problem

In the companion video, Maria identifies a potential $4.2M liquidity shortfall in week seven—driven by a concentration of supplier payments coinciding with delayed receivables from a major customer. Lisa asks:

"Alejandro, what's the best way to cover this shortfall?"

At this moment, Alejandro becomes an analytical engine that evaluates competing strategies across cost, timing, risk, and policy boundaries. He doesn't provide a single answer. He provides an optimized decision framework.

How Alejandro Thinks

Alejandro does not operate as a single model call.
He executes a multi-step optimization workflow orchestrated across several specialized reasoning modules:

1. Context Intake

Inputs received from orchestration:
- **Forecasted shortfall** — Amount ($4.2M), timing (Week 7, Day 3), duration (5 days)
- **Root cause analysis** — Maria's explanation of what's driving the gap
- **Risk indicators** — Confidence intervals, sensitivity to FX movements, dependency on uncertain inflows
- **Current positioning** — Cash balances by entity, currency exposure, existing commitments
- **Strategic context** — Upcoming M&A activity, dividend schedules, capital expenditure plans

Alejandro begins with a complete picture, not just a number.

2. Data Retrieval

Alejandro pulls structured, real-time data from multiple sources:

Internal sources:

- **Investment accounts** — Balances, maturity dates, liquidation costs, yield rates
- **Cash pools** — Notional pooling structures, physical pool balances, sweep arrangements
- **Credit facilities** — Available capacity, pricing tiers, covenant compliance status, utilization history
- **Intercompany balances** — Entity-level cash, transfer restrictions, tax implications, repatriation costs
- **Supplier payment schedules** — Upcoming obligations, early payment discount opportunities, payment term flexibility

External sources:

- **Interest rate curves** — Short-term borrowing costs, term structure, forward rates
- **FX projections** — Exchange rate forecasts for cross-border transfers
- **Funding market conditions** — Commercial paper rates, money market fund yields, repo availability

- **Counterparty data** — Bank relationship strength, credit facility covenants, supplier negotiation history

3. Scenario Modeling

Alejandro simulates multiple funding strategies simultaneously, each with full cost-benefit analysis:

Option A: Reallocate idle cash

Move $4.2M from low-yield money market investments in the U.S. entity to cover LATAM operations.
- **Cost impact:** Opportunity cost of 4.5% annual yield = ~$4,000 for 5-day period
- **Liquidity stability:** High—no new liabilities created
- **Risk exposure:** Minimal FX risk if hedged appropriately
- **Policy compliance:** ✓ Within buffer requirements

Option B: Draw revolving credit facility

Utilize $4.2M from existing $50M revolver with HSBC.
- **Cost impact:** Interest at SOFR + 150bps ≈ $1,200 for 5 days
- **Liquidity stability:** Medium—increases leverage ratio from 1.8x to 1.9x

- **Risk exposure:** Minimal—well within covenant thresholds
- **Policy compliance:** ✓ Below 40% utilization limit

Option C: Delay payments within policy limits

Extend DPO with Brazil supplier by 10 days, reducing immediate cash need to $2.5M.
- **Cost impact:** Foregone 2% early payment discount = $34,000
- **Liquidity stability:** Medium—shifts problem but doesn't solve it
- **Risk exposure:** Reputational risk with key supplier
- **Policy compliance:** ⚠ Requires VP approval for 60+ day extension

Option D: Intercompany funding transfer

Transfer $4.2M from European subsidiary with excess cash.
- **Cost impact:** FX conversion cost + withholding tax ≈ $18,000
- **Liquidity stability:** Medium—concentrates risk in EUR entity
- **Risk exposure:** Tax implications, potential repatriation restrictions
- **Policy compliance:** ✓ Subject to transfer pricing documentation

Option E: Short-term investment liquidation

Liquidate Treasury bills before maturity.
- **Cost impact:** Minimal market impact, ~$500 transaction cost
- **Liquidity stability:** High—but reduces investment portfolio diversification
- **Risk exposure:** Low
- **Policy compliance:** ✓ Within investment policy guidelines

Each scenario is evaluated across multiple dimensions with quantified trade-offs.

4. Policy Filtering

Before presenting options to Lisa, the orchestration layer applies treasury policies automatically:
- **Minimum liquidity buffers** — $10M per region (checked in real-time)
- **DPO limits** — Maximum 60 days without executive approval
- **Credit usage thresholds** — Revolver utilization capped at 40% without CFO sign-off
- **Risk exposure constraints** — Single-entity concentration limits, FX exposure caps
- **Counterparty limits** — Maximum exposure per banking relationship

Non-compliant options are either removed or flagged for exception approval.

In this case:
- Option C (delay payments) is flagged because it exceeds standard DPO policy
- All other options pass policy checks

5. Recommendation Generation

Only policy-compliant strategies are returned to Lisa, ranked by a composite score weighing cost, risk, and strategic alignment.

Alejandro's output:

*"Based on current conditions, I recommend **Option B: Draw $4.2M from the HSBC revolver**.*
Rationale:
- *Lowest all-in cost ($1,200 vs. $4,000+ for alternatives)*
- *Preserves investment portfolio positioning*
- *Maintains supplier relationships*
- *Keeps leverage within comfortable range (1.9x vs. 2.2x covenant)*
- *Execution time: < 2 hours*

*Alternative: **Option A** (reallocate idle cash) if you prefer zero leverage increase, though at higher opportunity cost.*

Option C requires VP approval due to DPO extension.»

These are recommendations—not actions. Lisa reviews, selects, and authorizes.

Liquidity Optimization Architecture
(Technical Blueprint)

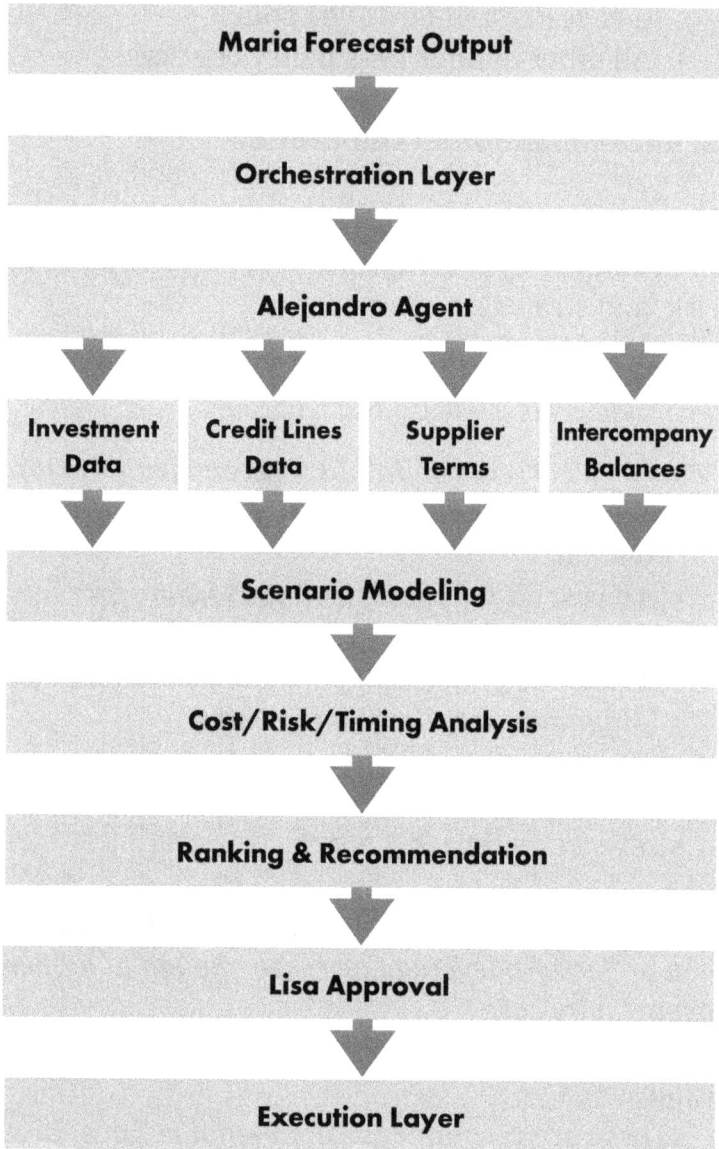

Maria Forecast Output

▼

Orchestration Layer

▼

Alejandro Agent

▼ ▼ ▼ ▼

| Investment Data | Credit Lines Data | Supplier Terms | Intercompany Balances |

▼ ▼ ▼ ▼

Scenario Modeling

▼

Cost/Risk/Timing Analysis

▼

Ranking & Recommendation

▼

Lisa Approval

▼

Execution Layer

Implementation Table — Alejandro's Workflow

Stage	Function	Example Technologies	Implementation Notes
Data Aggregation	Consolidate liquidity data	REST APIs, GraphQL, ETL pipelines	Real-time preferred; cached with 5-min TTL for performance
Optimization Engine	Evaluate scenarios	Python (SciPy, PuLP), PyTorch, AWS SageMaker	Can combine ML forecasting + rules-based constraints
Simulation Layer	Cost/risk comparison	Monte Carlo, deterministic models, sensitivity analysis	Explainable outputs required; no black-box optimization
Policy Engine	Governance filtering	Open Policy Agent, custom rules engine	Removes unsafe options; logs why options were filtered
Recommendation Generator	Human-readable output	LLM reasoning layer (GPT-4, Claude)	Must include rationale, trade-offs, and confidence levels
Execution Interface	Authorization & action	Treasury platform UI, bank APIs	Approval workflow with explainability context

Why Human Approval Matters

Alejandro can simulate thousands of scenarios instantly and identify the mathematically optimal solution.

But only Lisa:
- Understands strategic context — Is now the right time to use credit capacity given upcoming M&A plans?
- Owns institutional accountability — Will answer to the CFO and board for treasury decisions
- Holds authorization authority — Can override algorithmic recommendations based on judgment
- Knows relationship dynamics — Can assess whether extending DPO will damage a critical supplier relationship

The system is designed so that optimization accelerates decision-making without replacing judgment.

What This Changes

Traditional treasury liquidity management:
- Treasurer receives forecast
- Manually evaluates 2-3 options based on experience
- Makes decision with incomplete cost/risk data
- Execution takes hours to days

Agentic treasury liquidity management:
- System proactively surfaces shortfall
- Alejandro evaluates dozens of scenarios in seconds
- Treasurer sees complete trade-off analysis
- Decision made with confidence and full transparency
- Execution begins immediately after approval

Time from identification to action: **Minutes instead of days.**

Key Principle

Optimization without governance creates risk.
Agentic liquidity modeling only works when:
- **Policies are enforced automatically** — Non-compliant options never reach the decision-maker
- **Recommendations remain transparent** — Every suggestion includes explainable rationale
- **Humans authorize execution** — AI accelerates analysis; humans maintain accountability

This ensures treasury moves faster without losing control.

Alejandro doesn't make Lisa's job obsolete. He makes her exponentially more effective.

5. Sam: Real-Time Transaction Intelligence & Payment Verification

From Strategy to Execution

Maria forecasts risk. Alejandro optimizes liquidity. Sam ensures execution happens safely.

In modern treasury environments, timing is critical. Large outgoing payments often depend on incoming flows. A delay of minutes can create liquidity pressure or compliance risk. A missing confirmation can halt operations. An undetected duplicate payment can create accounting chaos.

Sam operates as the operational intelligence layer that connects treasury decision-making to real-time payment reality.

The Operational Scenario

In the companion video, Lisa needs to confirm whether an expected $7M payment from Costa Rica has arrived before authorizing a $5M supplier payment to a Brazilian vendor.

She asks:

"Sam, can you check the status of the transfer?"

Behind this simple request is a complex orchestration of payment visibility systems spanning multiple banks, payment networks, and time zones.

The Challenge Without Sam:

Lisa would need to:
- Log into three different bank portals
- Check SWIFT tracking manually
- Call the Costa Rica finance team to confirm initiation
- Wait for email confirmation from banking partners
- Cross-reference internal ledger entries
- Hope everything reconciles correctly

Time required: 30-60 minutes of manual work, with uncertainty until final settlement.

With Sam: The answer arrives in seconds, with complete context.

How Sam Works

Sam continuously monitors payment flows across multiple networks, operating as a real-time transaction intelligence system.

His workflow includes:

1. Real-Time Status Retrieval

Sam queries multiple data sources simultaneously:
- **Bank APIs** — Direct connection to treasury banks (HSBC, Citi, Santander) for account-level visibility
- **SWIFT gpi Tracker** — End-to-end payment tracking for cross-border wires, including intermediary banks
- **Instant payment rails** — FedNow (US), PIX (Brazil), SEPA Instant (Europe) for real-time settlement confirmation
- **ACH networks** — Same-day ACH status for domestic transfers
- **Internal treasury ledgers** — Expected payment schedule from ERP and TMS systems

For the Costa Rica payment, Sam determines:
- **Payment initiation time:** Yesterday, 4:47 PM EST
- **Current processing stage:** Cleared intermediary bank (Citibank), awaiting final settlement at receiving bank (Banco Nacional de Costa Rica)
- **Estimated settlement timing:** Today, 11:30 AM EST (based on historical patterns and current network status)
- **Current status:** In transit, no exceptions flagged

2. Reconciliation Intelligence

Sam compares expected flows against actual settlement data in real-time:

Expected incoming flows (from TMS):
- $7M from Costa Rica subsidiary — Due today
- $2.3M customer payment from Mexico — Due tomorrow
- $1.8M intercompany transfer from Chile — Due in 3 days

Actual settlement data (from bank feeds):
- $7M Costa Rica — Pending (current status: in transit)
- $450K customer payment — Settled (unexpected early payment)

Sam's reconciliation engine ensures:
- **No duplicate payments** — Detects if a payment ID appears twice across systems
- **No missing confirmations** — Flags expected payments that don't arrive within tolerance windows
- **Early detection of delays** — Compares actual timing against historical patterns; alerts if settlement is taking longer than usual
- **Exception identification** — Catches returned payments, partial settlements, or FX conversion discrepancies

3. Event Monitoring

Sam uses event-driven architecture rather than periodic polling:

- **Payment status changes trigger instant notifications** — When the Costa Rica payment status changes from "in transit" to "settled," Sam knows within seconds
- **Treasury receives updates automatically** — Push notifications to Treasury Platform, no manual checking required
- **No manual polling required** — System is reactive, not batch-based
- **Proactive alerting** — If a payment is delayed beyond expected windows, Sam alerts Lisa before she asks

Event examples:

- PAYMENT_INITIATED — $7M wire sent from Costa Rica
- INTERMEDIARY_CLEARED — Passed through Citibank correspondent
- SETTLEMENT_PENDING — Awaiting final credit
- PAYMENT_SETTLED — Funds available in receiving account
- PAYMENT_EXCEPTION — Unexpected delay or rejection

4. Coordination with Other Agents

Sam does not operate independently. He's integrated into the agentic treasury workflow.

If delays occur:

When Sam detects the Costa Rica payment is delayed beyond the expected 11:30 AM settlement window:

1. **Sam alerts orchestration layer** — "Expected $7M payment delayed; new ETA 2:45 PM"
2. **Orchestration evaluates impact** — Checks if this delay affects any pending obligations
3. **Alejandro is automatically triggered** — Begins evaluating short-term liquidity alternatives (use revolver? delay outgoing payment? reallocate funds?)
4. **Lisa receives integrated update** — Notification includes: payment delay details + Alejandro's recommended contingency options

Orchestration ensures coordination before presenting options to Lisa. She doesn't receive fragmented alerts from multiple agents—she receives a unified recommendation.

5. Human Confirmation

Once payment settles, Sam provides confirmation with complete context:

"The $7M transfer from Costa Rica has been credited to Account 4532 at 11:28 AM EST. Current available balance: $12.4M. You can proceed with the $5M supplier payment."

Execution proceeds only after human authorization.

Lisa clicks "Approve" in the Treasury Platform, and the $5M supplier payment initiates immediately—with Sam now tracking that outbound transfer.

Implementation Table — Sam's Technology Components

Capability	Function	Example Technologies	Implementation Notes
Payment Tracking	Real-time status monitoring	SWIFT gpi, FedNow APIs, bank partner APIs	Must support event-driven updates; webhooks preferred
Event Streaming	Instant state changes	Kafka, RabbitMQ, AWS EventBridge, Azure Event Grid	Low-latency architecture; sub-second processing

Transaction Intelligence Architecture (Technical Blueprint)

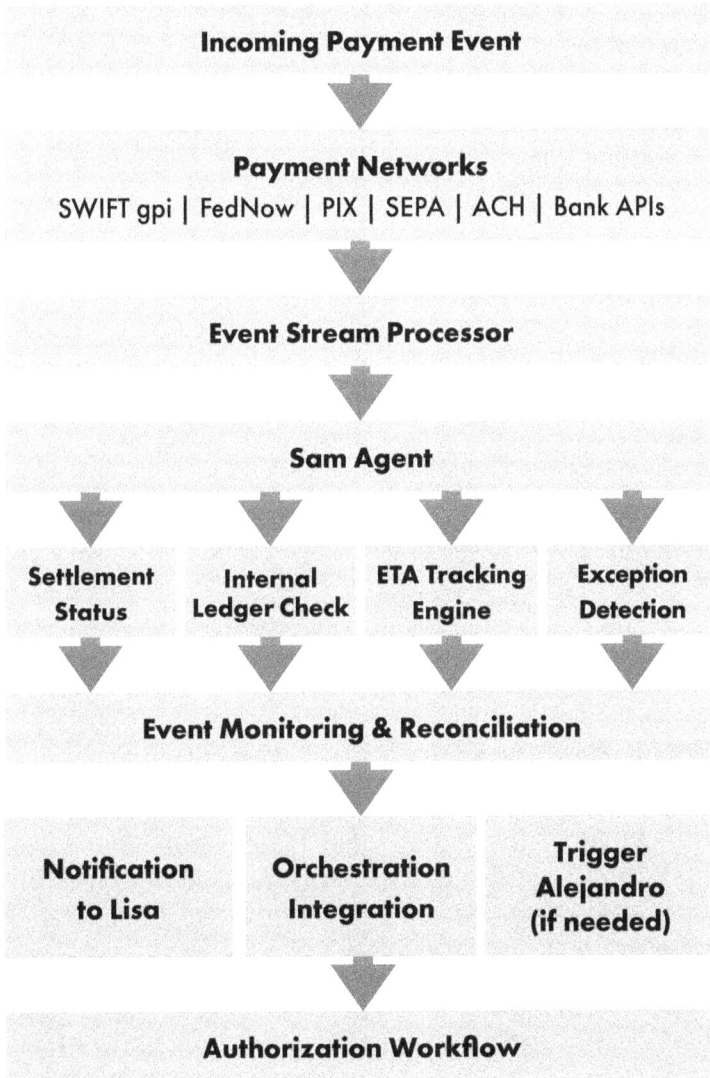

Incoming Payment Event

↓

Payment Networks
SWIFT gpi | FedNow | PIX | SEPA | ACH | Bank APIs

↓

Event Stream Processor

↓

Sam Agent

↓   ↓   ↓   ↓

| Settlement Status | Internal Ledger Check | ETA Tracking Engine | Exception Detection |

↓   ↓   ↓

Event Monitoring & Reconciliation

↓

| Notification to Lisa | Orchestration Integration | Trigger Alejandro (if needed) |

↓

Authorization Workflow

Capability	Function	Example Technologies	Implementation Notes
Reconciliation Engine	Expected vs actual comparison	Custom ledger logic, matching algorithms	Critical for accuracy; must handle partial settlements
ETA Prediction	Settlement timing forecasts	ML models trained on historical payment data	Improves as more data accumulates
Exception Detection	Anomaly identification	Rule-based + ML anomaly detection	Flags unusual delays, amounts, or routing
Notification Service	User alerts & updates	Webhooks, push notifications, Treasury UI integration	Context-aware; priority routing for urgent items
Authorization Flow	Human control gate	IAM + Treasury Platform UI	Role-based approvals; mobile-enabled for remote access

Why This Matters

Traditional treasury operations rely on:

- Manual checks across multiple banking portals
- Email confirmations that may be delayed or missed
- Batch reconciliation at end-of-day or even end-of-week
- Phone calls to banks or subsidiaries for status updates
- Uncertainty about whether funds are available

Agentic treasury replaces this with continuous operational awareness.

Sam provides:

✓ **Real-time visibility** — Know payment status instantly, across all networks
✓ **Reduced operational risk** — Catch exceptions before they cascade into bigger problems
✓ **Immediate settlement intelligence** — Execute decisions with confidence, not hope
✓ **Automatic escalation** — Issues are flagged and addressed proactively, not discovered later
✓ **Unified view** — One interface for all payment networks, banks, and currencies

The Impact in Practice:

Traditional Approach	Sam-Enabled Approach
"I'll check on that payment and get back to you in an hour"	"The payment settled 2 minutes ago; we can proceed"
End-of-day reconciliation reveals discrepancy	Real-time detection prevents downstream issues
Treasurer manually tracks 5 expected payments	Sam monitors continuously, alerts only when action needed
30-60 minutes per payment verification	5-10 seconds per payment verification

Key Principle

Execution intelligence does not remove humans.

It removes uncertainty.

Sam ensures Lisa acts with confidence because treasury has accurate, live operational truth.

Treasury professionals don't need to become experts in payment network infrastructure, SWIFT message types, or cross-border settlement timing. Sam handles the complexity. Lisa focuses on decisions.

This is the difference between reactive treasury and responsive treasury.

6. Human-in-the-Loop: Authorization, Control, and Governance

Intelligence Without Authority

Throughout the companion video, Maria, Alejandro, and Sam provide insights, recommendations, and operational updates.
Yet one principle remains constant:

They never execute decisions independently.

Every high-impact treasury action still requires Lisa's approval.
This is not a limitation.
It is the foundation of institutional trust.

Why Human Oversight Is Essential

Treasury operates within:
- Regulatory constraints
- Corporate governance frameworks
- Fiduciary responsibility
- Audit requirements

AI can accelerate analysis.
Only humans carry accountability.
The system is therefore designed so that:
- AI informs decisions
- Humans authorize execution

Where Human Approval Appears in the Workflow

In the video scenario, approval checkpoints occur at specific moments:

Liquidity Adjustment

Alejandro proposes reallocating funds.
Before execution:
→ Treasury Platform Prompt: **Authorization Required**
Lisa reviews and approves.

Risk Escalation

Maria detects a suspicious transaction pattern.
Before escalation:
→ Human authorization ensures governance alignment.

High-Value Payment Execution

Supplier payment exceeds approval threshold.
Maria signals:
"This transaction requires authorization."
Only after Lisa confirms does execution proceed.

Governance Architecture (Technical Blueprint)

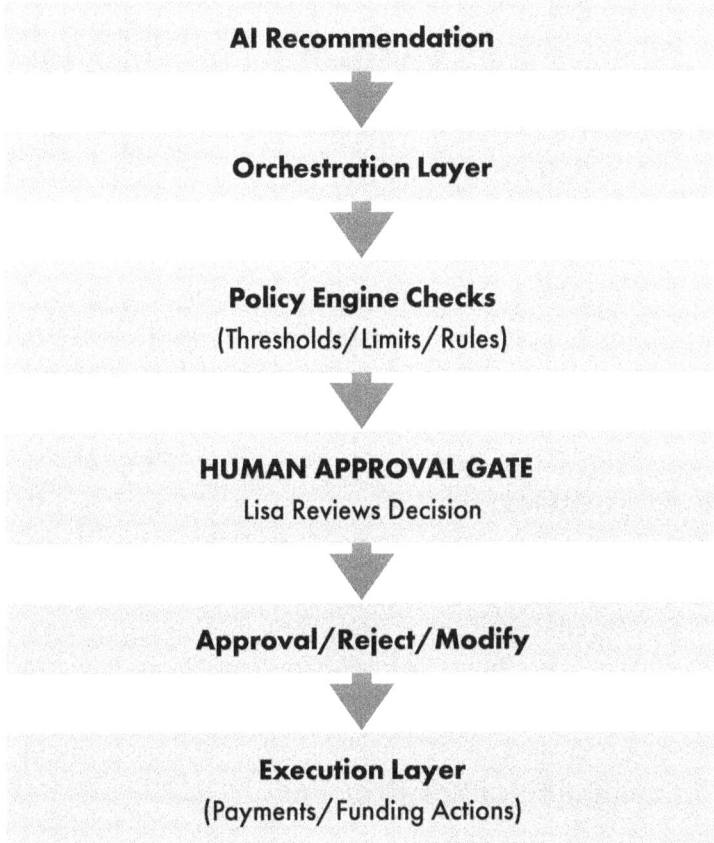

AI Recommendation

↓

Orchestration Layer

↓

Policy Engine Checks
(Thresholds/Limits/Rules)

↓

HUMAN APPROVAL GATE
Lisa Reviews Decision

↓

Approval/Reject/Modify

↓

Execution Layer
(Payments/Funding Actions)

Core Governance Mechanisms

1. Policy Enforcement Engine

Applies:
- Liquidity buffer rules
- Payment thresholds
- Counterparty risk limits
- Regulatory constraints

Policies are machine-enforced before humans even see recommendations.

2. Approval Matrix

Role-based controls define:
- Who can approve actions
- Approval levels by transaction size
- Escalation paths (e.g., CFO approval)

3. Explainability Requirements

Before approval, Lisa can view:
- Data sources used
- Reasoning summary
- Alternative options considered
- Risk implications

Transparency enables confident decision-making.

4. Immutable Audit Trail

Every decision records:
- Agent recommendation
- Data context
- Policy checks
- Human action

This supports:
- Audit reviews
- Compliance reporting
- Model governance

Implementation Table — Human Governance Controls

Control Mechanism	Purpose	Example Technologies	Implementation Notes
Policy Engine	Automatic rule enforcement	Open Policy Agent	Externalized policy configs
Role-Based Access	Approval hierarchy	IAM systems (Azure AD, Okta)	Treasury segregation of duties
Explainability Layer	Decision transparency	LLM reasoning logs	Required before approval

Control Mechanism	Purpose	Example Technologies	Implementation Notes
Audit Logging	Regulatory compliance	Splunk, ELK, Datadog	Immutable storage preferred
Workflow Approval	Human checkpoint	Treasury platform UI	Must be friction-light

Why This Changes Treasury

Traditional systems rely on manual compliance checks after decisions are made.

Agentic treasury embeds governance into the decision process itself.

This produces:

✓ Faster decisions

✓ Lower operational risk

✓ Stronger regulatory posture

✓ Greater confidence in AI recommendations

Key Principle

Human-in-the-loop is not about slowing AI down.

It is about ensuring intelligence operates within institutional accountability.

AI accelerates thinking.

Humans authorize action.

7. The Explainability Console: Making AI Decisions Transparent

Why Explainability Is Non-Negotiable

In institutional finance, a recommendation is not enough.

Treasury leaders must be able to answer:
- Why was this recommendation made?
- What data was used?
- Which assumptions were applied?
- What alternatives were considered?
- Which policies influenced the outcome?

Without explainability, AI becomes a black box.

In regulated environments, black boxes fail governance requirements.

The Explainability Console exists to ensure every AI-driven insight can be understood, challenged, and audited.

What the Explainability Console Does

The console is not a separate AI agent.

It is a transparency layer integrated into the orchestration system.

For every recommendation, it provides:

1. Data Traceability

Shows:
- Internal systems accessed (ERP, TMS, ledgers)
- External data sources used
- Timestamp of retrieved data

This confirms recommendations are grounded in real information.

2. Reasoning Summary

Explains:
- Why the agent chose a specific recommendation
- Which variables influenced the outcome
- Key trade-offs considered

This allows treasury professionals to validate logic.

3. Policy Context

Displays:
- Rules applied by governance engine
- Thresholds checked
- Constraints that removed alternative options

Lisa sees what the system rejected and why.

4. Scenario Comparison

Shows alternative paths considered.
  Example:
  • Reallocate funds (selected)
  • Draw credit facility (alternative)
  • Delay payments (policy-limited)

  Decision transparency builds confidence.

5. Approval History

Records:
  • Human decisions
  • Overrides
  • Timestamped authorization actions

  Every outcome remains auditable.

Explainability Architecture
(Technical Blueprint)

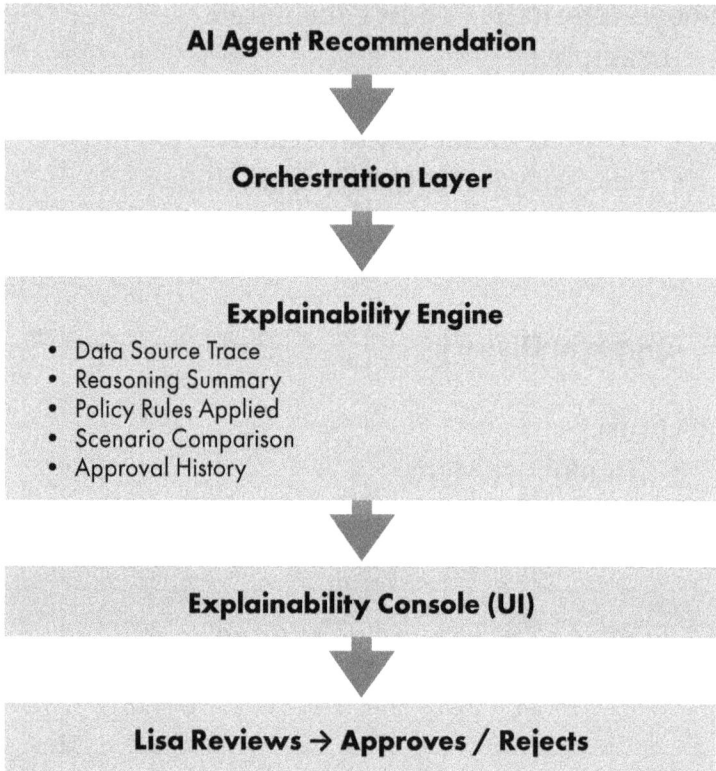

AI Agent Recommendation

▼

Orchestration Layer

▼

Explainability Engine

- Data Source Trace
- Reasoning Summary
- Policy Rules Applied
- Scenario Comparison
- Approval History

▼

Explainability Console (UI)

▼

Lisa Reviews → Approves / Rejects

Implementation Table — Explainability Components

Capability	Function	Example Technologies	Implementation Notes
Reasoning Logs	Capture model rationale	Structured LLM logging	Store prompts + outputs
Data Trace Engine	Show data lineage	Metadata tracking systems	Must include timestamps
Policy Transparency	Display applied rules	Policy engine integration	Human-readable output required
Scenario Viewer	Compare options	Simulation logs	Essential for governance
Audit Interface	Review approvals	Treasury UI dashboard	Role-based visibility

What Lisa Sees in Practice

Before approving a high-value action, Lisa can inspect:
- Forecast assumptions used by Maria
- Liquidity simulations run by Alejandro
- Payment status validation from Sam
- Policies that triggered authorization requirements

She is not asked to trust the system blindly.
She is empowered to understand it.

Why This Matters for Institutions

The Explainability Console transforms AI from:

✗ Automation risk

 into

✓ Controlled institutional intelligence

 It enables:
 - Regulatory confidence
 - Internal audit acceptance
 - Executive transparency
 - Faster decision approvals

Key Principle

Explainability is not a feature.
 It is the foundation of trust between humans and intelligent systems.
 Without transparency, collaboration fails.
 With transparency, AI becomes institutional infrastructure.

8. End-to-End Operational Flow: Human and AI Working as One Treasury System

From Architecture to Daily Operations

By this stage, the system contains:
- Orchestration control
- Agentic RAG intelligence
- Liquidity optimization logic
- Real-time transaction monitoring
- Human authorization gates
- Explainability and auditability

Page 9 shows how these elements operate together as a continuous treasury workflow.

The goal is not automation of tasks.

The goal is orchestration of intelligence.

The Operational Sequence

The following steps occur continuously in the background of Lisa's day.

Step 1 — Human Intent

Lisa initiates interaction:
  "Show me our projected cash flow for the next 90 days."
  The request enters the Treasury Platform.

Step 2 — Orchestration Activation

The orchestration layer:
  • Classifies intent
  • Routes request to Maria
  • Determines required data sources
  • Applies policy context

  No agent acts independently.

Step 3 — Intelligence Generation

Maria uses Agentic RAG to:
  • Retrieve enterprise and market data
  • Generate forecast projections
  • Detect liquidity risks

  Output is structured and explainable.

Step 4 — Optimization Workflow

Liquidity shortfall detected.
  Orchestration automatically engages Alejandro.

He:
- Simulates funding strategies
- Filters options through policies
- Produces optimized recommendations

Lisa reviews options via explainability console.

Step 5 — Transaction Coordination

Lisa requests payment verification.
Sam:
- Queries payment networks
- Tracks settlement status
- Synchronizes with internal ledgers
- Notifies Lisa when funds settle

If delays occur, orchestration re-engages Alejandro automatically.

Step 6 — Human Approval

Before execution:
- Policy engine triggers authorization gate
- Explainability context is displayed
- Lisa approves or modifies action

Human authority remains central.

Step 7 — Secure Execution

Once approved:
- Execution layer processes transactions
- Compliance logging occurs automatically
- Audit trail updates in real time

Implementation Table — End-to-End Workflow Mapping

Operational Phase	Primary Actor	System Responsibility	Control Mechanism
Intent Capture	Lisa	Define business need	Human authority
Routing & Governance	Orchestration	Coordinate agents	Policy enforcement
Forecasting	Maria	Predict liquidity risk	Grounded data retrieval
Optimization	Alejandro	Evaluate funding strategies	Simulation + policy filter
Transaction Monitoring	Sam	Validate settlement reality	Real-time data tracking
Decision Approval	Lisa	Authorize action	Human-in-the-loop
Execution	Platform	Process transaction	Governance + audit

End-to-End Operational Blueprint

Lisa (Human Treasurer)

▼

Treasury Platform Interface

▼

ORCHESTRATION CONTROL PLANE

- Intent Routing
- Workflow Coordination
- Policy Enforcement
- Audit Tracking

▼

AI AGENT COLLABORATION
Maria → Alejandro → Sam

▼

Data Retrieval & Reasoning
(Agentic RAG + LLM)

▼

Explainability Console

▼

Human Approval Gate

▼

Execution & Compliance Systems

What This Operational Model Changes

Traditional treasury:
- Sequential processes
- Human coordination between systems
- Delayed awareness

Agentic treasury:
✓ Continuous intelligence loop
✓ Automatic coordination between agents
✓ Instant operational visibility
✓ Governance embedded into flow

Treasury becomes adaptive rather than reactive.

Key Principle

The system does not automate decisions.
It orchestrates intelligence so that humans make better decisions faster.
Lisa is not replaced.
She becomes amplified.

9. Deployment Roadmap: Building an Agentic Treasury Platform

From Concept to Institutional Reality

The architecture shown throughout this guide is not deployed all at once.

Successful institutions implement agentic treasury systems incrementally, prioritizing governance and operational stability over automation speed.

The goal is not to "install AI."

The goal is to evolve treasury into an intelligent operating model.

Phase 1 — Establish the Control Plane

Before deploying agents, organizations must build orchestration and governance foundations.

Key Objectives

- Implement orchestration layer
- Define treasury policies as machine-enforceable rules
- Enable centralized audit logging
- Integrate core authentication and approval workflows

Deliverables

✓ Workflow orchestration engine
✓ Policy enforcement framework
✓ Approval hierarchy integration
✓ Basic observability dashboards

This phase enables safe experimentation.

Phase 2 — Connect Enterprise Data

Intelligence cannot exist without grounded data.

Key Objectives

- Integrate ERP and TMS systems
- Connect bank APIs
- Establish unified data access layer
- Prepare vectorized knowledge storage for RAG

Deliverables

✓ Data connectors and pipelines
✓ Historical data warehouse access
✓ Market data integrations
✓ Policy repositories accessible to AI

This creates the data foundation for trusted reasoning.

Phase 3 — Deploy First Agent (Maria)

Start with forecasting and risk.
   Why:
   • Low operational risk
   • High strategic value
   • Immediate visibility gains

Key Objectives

   • Deploy Agentic RAG pipeline
   • Integrate forecasting engine
   • Introduce explainability interface
   • Maintain human approvals

Expected Outcomes

✓ Improved forecast accuracy
✓ Early risk visibility
✓ Increased treasury confidence in AI outputs

Phase 4 — Add Optimization Intelligence (Alejandro)

Once forecasting becomes trusted, optimization can be introduced.

Key Objectives

- Deploy scenario simulation models
- Integrate liquidity decision engines
- Apply policy constraints automatically

Expected Outcomes

✓ Faster funding decisions
✓ Reduced liquidity inefficiencies
✓ Policy-driven recommendations

Phase 5 — Add Operational Intelligence (Sam)

Transaction intelligence is introduced after governance maturity.

Key Objectives

- Integrate payment network APIs
- Deploy event-driven monitoring
- Enable real-time alerts and reconciliation

Expected Outcomes

✓ Live settlement visibility
✓ Reduced operational risk
✓ Faster execution confidence

Deployment Roadmap (Visual Blueprint)

Phase 1 → Orchestration & Governance

Phase 2 → Data Integration

Phase 3 → Forecasting Agent (Maria)

Phase 4 → Liquidity Optimization (Alejandro)

Phase 5 → Transaction Intelligence (Sam)

Phase 6 → Fully Orchestrated Agentic Treasury

Phase 6 — Full Agentic Orchestration

Final stage integrates all capabilities.
The orchestration layer now:
- Coordinates agents automatically
- Synchronizes workflows
- Maintains full explainability

At this stage treasury evolves into an adaptive intelligence system.

Implementation Table — Recommended Rollout Strategy

Phase	Focus	Primary Technology Area	Risk Level
1	Governance Foundation	Orchestration + IAM	Low
2	Data Connectivity	APIs + Data Platform	Medium
3	Forecasting Intelligence	RAG + LLM	Low
4	Liquidity Optimization	Simulation models	Medium
5	Transaction Monitoring	Event-driven systems	Medium
6	Full Orchestration	Integrated AI ecosystem	Controlled

What Institutions Learn

Organizations that succeed follow one principle:

Governance first. Intelligence second. Automation last.

The sequence matters.

Deploying AI before governance creates risk.

Deploying governance first creates trust.

Final Perspective

The future of treasury is not defined by autonomous systems.
 It is defined by collaboration between:
- Human judgment
- Institutional governance
- Intelligent orchestration

Lisa remains the treasurer.
 Maria, Alejandro, and Sam become permanent members of her operating environment — always present, always explainable, always accountable to human authority.

Closing Thought

The agentic treasury is not a destination.
 It is a new operating model where institutions evolve from:
- Periodic decisions → continuous intelligence
- Static processes → adaptive workflows
- Human-only teams → human-AI collaboration

The question is no longer whether treasury will adopt intelligent systems.
 The question is how deliberately it will be built.

The Path Forward for
Agentic Institutional Treasury

We began with Lisa, the corporate treasurer confronting a reality where volatility moves faster than reporting cycles, where liquidity risks emerge between closing reports, and where market signals shift before committees can convene. We saw her working alongside Maria, Alejandro, and Sam: three AI agents who transformed her capacity to respond to this complexity. But as the video made clear, this was not about digital assistants responding to prompts. It was about infrastructure.

Throughout this field guide, we have deconstructed that infrastructure: the orchestration layer that coordinates intelligence, the Agentic RAG system that grounds recommendations in enterprise data, the policy engine that enforces governance automatically, and the human approval gates that preserve institutional authority. What appeared in the video as seamless collaboration revealed itself to be a carefully architected system where every layer serves a specific purpose and every decision point maintains human accountability.

The gap between analysis and action, which has become a source of exposure for modern treasury operations, closes not through speed alone but through the orchestration of intelligence. Maria's forecasts don't just inform Lisa; they automatically trigger Alejandro's optimization workflows when shortfalls emerge. Sam's payment monitoring doesn't just provide visibility; it integrates with liquidity planning so that execution timing reflects settlement reality. The system operates as continuous intelligence, not periodic reporting, because the orchestration layer synchronizes agents, data sources, and policy constraints in real time.

This represents a fundamental shift in how treasury operates. Reactive becomes predictive not because AI can forecast the future, but because Maria identifies liquidity gaps weeks before they materialize, giving Lisa time to act rather than react. Manual becomes automated not by eliminating human judgment, but by removing the hours spent gathering data from disconnected systems, reconciling inconsistencies, and building spreadsheets, allowing Lisa to focus on strategic decisions rather than operational logistics. Transactional becomes strategic because the operational complexity is handled by orchestrated intelligence, elevating Lisa's role from process manager to risk owner, from solo operator to team leader, from reactive analyst to proactive strategist.

But this transformation only works when built on seven architectural principles that have threaded through every section of this guide. Governance comes before intelligence. The orchestration layer must be production-ready before the first agent goes live, with policies codified and approval matrices defined. Recommendations must be grounded in evidence. Agentic RAG ensures every insight traces back to real enterprise data, not training memory. The system is transparent by design. The Explainability Console makes every recommendation inspectable, allowing Lisa to view data sources, reasoning steps, and alternatives considered. Human authority is preserved. High-value payments require approval, liquidity adjustments require authorization, and risk escalations require judgment. Treasury policies function as code, automatically filtering non-compliant options before they reach decision-makers. The system provides continuous intelligence. Sam monitors payments in real-time, Maria updates forecasts as conditions change, and Alejandro re-evaluates scenarios when new information arrives. And finally, the architecture fails safely. When uncertainty arises, control escalates to humans rather than proceeding autonomously.

The deployment journey we've outlined reflects how institutions move from the treasury of today to the treasury Lisa operates within. Organizations begin by establishing the control plane, proving that governance can be embedded into AI systems rather than layered on afterward. They connect enterprise data, demonstrating that intelligence can be grounded in institutional truth. They deploy Maria first, showing that forecasting and risk analysis can become both more accurate and more explainable.

They add Alejandro's optimization, proving that scenario modeling can accelerate decisions while respecting policy constraints. They integrate Sam's operational intelligence, eliminating the payment uncertainty that historically delayed execution. And finally, they achieve full orchestration, where Maria, Alejandro, and Sam collaborate automatically while Lisa retains ultimate authority.

The sequence matters because organizations that rush to deploy agents before establishing governance create the very risks this architecture is designed to prevent: ungoverned AI, hallucination risk, and loss of institutional control. Organizations that over-engineer governance before demonstrating value lose institutional momentum. The path forward requires deliberate governance paired with pragmatic deployment: governance first, intelligence second, automation last.

For treasury professionals, this changes everything and nothing. Lisa remains the treasurer. She remains accountable. She remains the decision-maker. But she is no longer alone, no longer reacting, no longer constrained by the speed of manual analysis. She has become exponentially more capable, not because AI replaced her judgment, but because AI amplified her capacity to exercise it. The role elevates from data gatherer to decision architect, from reactive analyst to proactive strategist, from solo operator to team leader. The accountability intensifies. The impact multiplies.

For the organization, the benefits extend far beyond treasury. Improved liquidity management, enhanced risk mitigation, accelerated decision cycles, stronger governance posture, and scalability without headcount growth: these operational improvements compound over time into strategic advantage. But more importantly, the agentic treasury model represents a pattern that will spread across the enterprise. The same architecture of orchestration, specialized agents, grounded intelligence, and human authority applies to FP&A, financial reporting, tax planning, capital allocation, procurement, supply chain, HR, legal, and compliance. Early adopters gain competitive advantage. As the model proves itself, it becomes table stakes.

The institutions that build agentic systems deliberately, with governance, transparency, and human authority embedded from the start, will lead this transformation. Those that delay will find themselves outpaced by competitors who make faster decisions with greater confidence. But building responsibly requires addressing fundamental questions of accountability, bias, transparency, privacy, and security. These are not compliance checkboxes but design requirements embedded into the architecture from the beginning.

Many technology vendors now market "AI-powered treasury solutions," but the questions this guide has raised provide a framework for evaluation. Where is the orchestration layer? How is intelligence grounded? What policy enforcement exists? How is explainability implemented? Where does human authority sit? What audit capabilities exist? These questions separate systems built on the principles in this guide from tools that add AI features without institutional control.

Looking ahead, the timeline appears clear. Leading institutions are deploying pilots now. By 2027, multi-agent coordination will mature. By 2030, agentic treasury becomes expected capability. Beyond 2031, these systems extend into integrated financial operations. But what remains constant is the direction of travel: treasury operations are becoming more intelligent, more integrated, and more dependent on AI capabilities. The question is not whether to adapt, but how deliberately to do so.

Technology does not dictate outcomes. Choices do. The same AI capabilities that enable responsible agentic treasury could enable systems that obscure accountability, execute decisions without oversight, and operate as black boxes. The architecture presented in this guide represents a choice: to build AI systems that preserve human authority, enforce institutional governance, demand transparency, and maintain accountability. As treasury professionals, technology leaders, and institutional decision-makers build agentic systems, they face a fundamental choice: design for control or accept loss of control by default. The control plane matters more than the intelligence layer. The governance framework matters more than the optimization algorithm. The human approval gate matters more than the speed of automation.

The companion video showed Lisa working alongside Maria, Alejandro, and Sam. But beneath that interaction lies the orchestration layer that coordinates intelligence, enforces policy, maintains audit trails, and preserves human authority. Beneath the orchestration layer lies the Agentic RAG system that grounds recommendations in enterprise data. Beneath the data layer lies the governance framework that defines accountability, transparency, and control. The system works because every layer serves its purpose. Remove orchestration, and you have ungoverned AI. Remove data grounding, and you have hallucination risk. Remove human authority, and you have institutional liability.

The agentic treasury is not about making treasury autonomous. It is about making treasury intelligent without sacrificing control. The precision that has always defined treasury operations now operates at the speed of volatility. The gap between analysis and action, which opened as markets accelerated beyond human response time, closes through orchestrated intelligence that amplifies human judgment rather than replacing it.

This is the promise of agentic treasury: human judgment at machine speed, institutional intelligence under human authority, and strategic capability that scales without sacrificing control.

The institutions that build toward this vision deliberately (with governance first, intelligence second, and automation last) will define the future of treasury operations.

The future is not autonomous. The future is augmented. And it begins with the choice to build responsibly.

Appendix:

FRAMEWORKS AND TOOLKITS

This appendix offers practical implementation guidance for enterprise leaders, architects, and operational teams building agentic systems within financial institutions. Each framework in this section is designed to translate strategy into execution, grounded in real-world platforms, operational models, and regulatory considerations. Use this appendix as a reference during planning, design sprints, quarterly reviews, or capability building sessions.

These tools align with the core elements introduced throughout the book, particularly in the domains of readiness, model architecture, governance, workflow design, deployment patterns, performance measurement, and talent activation. Together, they serve as a system-wide blueprint for operationalizing agentic banking.

1. Agentic Readiness Assessment

This framework helps you evaluate your institution's maturity across four foundational pillars: data infrastructure, model strategy, organizational alignment, and governance and risk. It is a starting point to surface where your institution is prepared to adopt agentic capabilities and where foundational investments are still needed.

Use this framework when launching transformation initiatives, prior to agent deployment or as part of quarterly capability assessments. The outcome is a shared baseline to guide strategic prioritization and execution.

Assess each of the following dimensions:
- **Data Infrastructure**: Can your teams securely access and connect real-time, composable data across silos?
- **Model Strategy**: Are models deployed, evaluated, and tuned with business alignment and explainability in mind?

- **Organizational Alignment**: Are workflows designed to support human-agent collaboration with proper training and oversight?
- **Governance and Risk**: Are auditability, override logic, and policy alignment embedded in your AI lifecycle?

Stakeholders typically include the CDO, CTO, AI leads, heads of compliance, innovation officers, and enterprise architects.

Implementation steps include conducting a readiness workshop across key functions, scoring each pillar on a scale of one to five, flagging red and yellow zones for remediation, and building a quarterly roadmap to close capability gaps.

Use the following diagnostic prompts to guide the discussion:
- What agentic workflows are currently unsupported by data pipelines?
- Where is human intervention still required in repetitive decision loops?
- Do current governance systems allow for override logging and escalation?
- Are operational teams designing with agent participation in mind?

Use a prioritization grid to classify readiness based on impact and feasibility, enabling teams to focus on high-readiness, high-impact opportunities first, while planning for longer-term capability building in lower-maturity areas.

2. Model Fit Matrix

Selecting the appropriate model architecture is essential to aligning business objectives, risk constraints, and operational needs. This framework helps teams match model types to use cases based on performance, explainability, speed, and integration requirements.

Use this matrix during AI initiative planning, model governance reviews, or prior to agent deployment. It supports data science leads, risk teams, and operational owners in choosing models that are technically feasible, explainable, and regulatory-aligned.

Model-to-Use Case Alignment

Use Case	Model Type	Key Considerations
FX Forecasting	Fine-tuned LLM + Time Series Ensemble	Needs fast inference, T+1 data, traceability
Compliance Escalation	Multi-agent with rule overlay	Requires explainability, override logic

Use Case	Model Type	Key Considerations
Client Sentiment Analysis	Embedding-- based LLM	Best for language diversity, customer nuance
Treasury Cash Ops	Retrieval-- augmented LLM	Structured triggers, contextual reasoning
Agent-- Aided CX	Dialogue-- optimized LLM	Handles multi-turn interactions, multilingual input

Use Case Commentary

- **FX Forecasting**: In fast-moving currency environments, treasury agents often rely on time-series forecasting supported by LLM overlays for commentary generation and anomaly detection. These models must support low-latency inference and integrate with ERP and external market feeds.
- **Compliance Escalation**: When agents act within risk or regulatory contexts, decision-- making must be explainable. Multi-agent systems layered with rule-based logic allow for overrides, thresholds, and audit-ready transparency.
- **Client Sentiment Analysis**: Embedding-- based LLMs interpret language tone, frequency, and emotional markers across client touchpoints. They're ideal for RAG-style

memory systems and multilingual sentiment extraction.

- **Treasury Cash Ops**: Retrieval-augmented models enhance real-time visibility into working capital decisions. These agents access structured internal sources (T+1 positions, thresholds, policy documents) and respond to events such as forecast gaps or liquidity shocks.
- **Agent-Aided CX**: In client-facing interactions, agents powered by fine-tuned LLMs manage conversations across multiple languages and intents. These agents act as first-response layers, augmenting service teams while learning from feedback over time.

Diagnostic prompts include:
- What are the latency or transparency requirements for this use case?
- Can this model be retrained easily or should it be wrapped with governance rules?
- Is this workflow subject to regulatory scrutiny or discretionary judgment?
- Are the outputs assistive, suggestive, or autonomous?

Start with conservative model selection in regulated domains, and increase model autonomy as trust, audit controls, and performance maturity evolve.

3. Governance Activation Framework

Agentic systems challenge traditional governance models. They act with speed, adapt based on feedback, and often operate at the edge of compliance thresholds. This framework helps institutional leaders establish oversight, transparency, and accountability from design to deployment.

Use this framework during early-stage design, pilot deployment, or system audits. It is most effective when applied collaboratively between product, risk, compliance, engineering, and legal teams.

Governance must be embedded into the agent lifecycle, not bolted on after deployment. This includes clarity around ownership, observability, override controls, and regulatory alignment.

Governance Layers

Layer	Focus Area	Institutional Owner
Oversight	Ownership, decision rights, escalation maps	Risk committees, AI councils
Transparency	Action logging, visibility, memory retention	Engineering, Internal Audit
Accountability	Override controls, thresholds, intervention paths	Ops Risk, Legal, Governance Ops
Regulatory Alignment	Compliance mapping, audit triggers, reporting	Regulatory Affairs, Internal Audit

Implementation Guidance

Oversight: Assign domain ownership for each agent and ensure decision rights are clearly documented. Establish escalation protocols and governance charters across business and technology.

Transparency: All agent actions should be observable through logs and dashboards. Design memory policies in advance, how long information is retained, where it is stored, and who has access.

Accountability: Define what triggers an override, who can intervene, and how these events are recorded. Ensure actions taken by agents are traceable and reversible when needed.

Regulatory Alignment: Map system behaviors to frameworks such as Basel III, MiFID II, and GDPR. Maintain internal control libraries and prepare for both internal and external audits.

Diagnostic prompts include:

- Which agents are currently operating without assigned business or risk owners?
- How are overrides triggered, and how frequently do they occur?
- What percentage of agent decisions are logged with complete audit trails?
- Where do regulatory requirements conflict with agent autonomy?

Governance must evolve with the system. Conduct quarterly reviews of all deployed agents, flag drift from approved behaviors, and ensure any new models go through pre-defined compliance gates before deployment.

4. Agentic Journey Design Canvas

Designing with agents requires a shift from static workflows to adaptive decision environments. The Agentic Journey Design Canvas is a structured tool for mapping how intelligent agents interact with people, data, and governance layers in specific business contexts.

Use this canvas during product sprints, operational design sessions, or workflow modernization initiatives. It is especially useful when co-creating journeys across business, AI, and UX teams.

The goal is to define the agent's role, its triggers, its data sources, and its constraints, so that human trust, system performance, and regulatory clarity are built in from the start.

Canvas Fields

Component	Key Design Focus
Persona	Define the user interacting with or supported by the agent
Intent	Clarify the business goal driving the workflow
Agent Role	Describe whether the agent monitors, recommends, or takes action

Component	Key Design Focus
Trigger	Identify the events or thresholds that activate the agent
Data Sources	List what information the agent needs to perform
Governance Layer	Define the constraints, policies, and risk limits applied
Feedback Loop	Explain how the agent learns or adapts over time

Example Use Case

- **Persona**: Lisa, Head of Liquidity
- **Intent**: Preemptively mitigate short-term cash shortfalls
- **Agent Role**: Monitor account flows, recommend sweeps, escalate exceptions
- **Trigger**: Forecasted gap in cash coverage beyond threshold
- **Data Sources**: ERP system, market volatility feeds, policy buffers
- **Governance Layer**: Basel compliance, internal cash limits, override rules
- **Feedback Loop**: Overrides by Lisa are logged, triggering model retraining on thresholds

Implementation Guidance

Start by identifying a workflow where agents can augment or automate high-friction decision points.

Then, in a cross-functional session, work through each canvas field to define what the agent sees, does, and reacts to. Ensure governance stakeholders are present to set escalation and intervention logic.

Use the canvas again after pilot deployment to review what worked, what failed, and where adjustments are needed, especially in feedback loops and risk constraints.

Diagnostic prompts include:

- Is the agent interrupting or integrating into the existing workflow?
- Does the agent have access to relevant data with the necessary latency and granularity?
- Are override pathways intuitive, logged, and respected by the system?
- How does agent learning occur, and who validates that it's aligned with business goals?

The canvas transforms abstract AI capability into operational clarity. It allows teams to design with intention and govern with foresight.

5. Deployment Patterns

Deploying agentic systems is not only a technical choice, it is a strategic decision that shapes how intelligence is distributed, governed, and evolved across the enterprise. This framework outlines the four most common deployment modes and when to use them.

Use this guide during architecture planning, solution design, or platform selection. It is particularly valuable when aligning business leaders, product teams, and technology functions around scalability, latency, and governance trade-offs.

The right deployment mode depends on system complexity, regulatory needs, and operational structure.

Deployment Modes

Pattern	Description	Best Fit Use Cases
Embedded Agent	Deployed directly within existing products or systems	Task automation, CX augmentation, internal tools
Orchestrated Agent	Connects actions across multiple platforms and systems	Treasury workflows, compliance, fraud detection
Federated Agent	Distributed across regions or business lines under shared policy	Global FX desks, local compliance agents
Shadow Agent	Runs parallel to existing systems for monitoring or simulation	Model training, internal sandboxes, safe piloting

Embedded Agents integrate tightly into user-facing systems, often operating within ERPs, CRMs, or operational tools. These are well-suited for tasks where latency is low and context is local, such as suggesting payment routing paths or flagging exceptions in real time. Their main limitation is scalability across domains.

Orchestrated Agents act as coordinators across disparate systems. For example, in treasury, an orchestrated agent might pull data from TMS, market feeds, and policy engines to guide intraday cash decisions. These require robust observability and coordination tooling.

Federated Agents allow for autonomy at the business-unit level, with centralized governance. Common in global banks, this pattern supports local innovation while ensuring alignment with enterprise-level controls. Challenges include version control and oversight consistency.

Shadow Agents observe but do not intervene. Used in pilot phases or regulatory testing, they are essential for understanding agent behavior, training models, and building trust. Because they don't affect production workflows, they are low-risk environments for iteration.

Diagnostic prompts include:

- Does the agent operate across one system or many?
- How quickly must the agent act, and who must review its actions?
- What governance tools are needed for monitoring, override, and escalation?
- How do we test this agent before exposing it to customers or regulators?

Deploy conservatively in high-risk domains. Use shadow or embedded models first, then scale to orchestrated or federated designs as maturity increases.

6. Metrics That Matter

Measuring agent performance is essential, not just for optimization, but for trust, compliance, and enterprise alignment. This framework outlines the key performance indicators (KPIs) that matter across technical, operational, and governance layers.

Use this during pilot phases, quarterly reviews, or executive reporting. These metrics help teams assess impact, detect drift, and align system behavior with business outcomes and regulatory expectations.

Each metric serves a different phase in the agentic lifecycle, from deployment readiness to post-launch performance.

Key Metric Categories

Category	KPI	Purpose
Adoption & Coverage	Percentage of agent-- augmented workflows	Tracks transformation depth and scope
	Number of active agents across business units	Monitors scale and reach

Category	KPI	Purpose
Model Performance	Latency, accuracy, hallucination rate	Evaluates response quality and risk
	Feedback incorporation rate	Tracks how quickly systems adapt and learn
Governance & Trust	Override frequency, audit completeness	Indicates trust, transparency, and compliance readiness
Business Impact	Reduction in time-to-decision, NPS delta	Links system performance to client or operational value

Implementation Guidance

Start by defining success metrics per use case before launch. For a treasury forecasting agent, for example, time-to-insight and override frequency might be the primary measures. For a compliance agent, transparency and audit log completeness take priority.

Integrate metric tracking into observability stacks using dashboards, log systems, or human feedback interfaces. Establish regular reviews, monthly at the team level, quarterly at the governance and executive level.

Diagnostic prompts include:

- Are agents making decisions faster than human teams with acceptable accuracy?
- Where are overrides most frequent, and are they tied to model drift or governance gaps?

- Are audit logs complete, structured, and accessible to compliance?
- How do agent decisions correlate with changes in operational KPIs or client satisfaction?

The right metrics align stakeholders. Business owners track impact, engineers monitor quality, and governance teams ensure control. Metrics are not just for dashboards, they are for decisions.

7. Talent Activation Guide

Agentic transformation is not just a shift in technology, it's a shift in roles, responsibilities, and institutional mindset. This guide outlines the key roles required to build, govern, and evolve agentic systems at scale.

Use this during transformation planning, hiring, upskilling, or organizational design. It helps leadership teams identify where current capabilities can be expanded and where new roles must be developed or recruited.

Each role plays a specific part in making agents safe, effective, and adaptive.

Core Roles and Capabilities

Role	Focus Area	Required Skills
Agent Trainer	Tuning prompts, refining behavior	NLP, business context, LLM usage
Governance Ops Lead	Policy enforcement, audit paths	Risk, compliance, operations
Orchestration Engineer	Integrating agent actions across systems	APIs, data flows, workflow tools
Agentic Experience Designer	Workflow co-design, human-agent interfaces	UX, service design, Figma or equivalent
AI Risk Officer	Oversight, alignment to regulation	Risk frameworks, legal fluency
Feedback Analyst	Measuring agent effectiveness and drift	Analytics, behavioral insights, override analysis

Implementation Guidance

In early stages, many of these roles may be shared or hybrid. For example, a product manager might also serve as an agent trainer or feedback analyst. As systems scale, formalizing these roles ensures long-term continuity and resilience.

Partner with HR to map skills to job architecture. Where needed, develop upskilling programs focused on AI literacy, prompt design, governance tooling, or compliance automation.

Form cross-functional pods around major use cases, for instance, treasury agents should be co-developed by liquidity experts, orchestration engineers, and governance leads.

Diagnostic prompts include:

- Do we have internal capabilities to fine-tune and monitor agent behavior?
- Who owns the escalation map for each agent's decisions?
- Are business stakeholders part of the workflow design and feedback loop?
- Where do we need to reskill, and where must we hire new talent?

Talent is the control layer of the agentic enterprise. The best systems are built not just by algorithms, but by teams who understand when to let go, when to override, and how to evolve the agent's role over time.

8. Convergence Toolkit: Agentic AI Meets Programmable Finance

As AI agents evolve into institutional decision-makers and programmable finance reshapes execution, convergence is no longer a theoretical frontier—it's becoming operational reality. The fusion of reasoning (AI) and verification (blockchain) allows institutions to shift from intent to action with both speed and verifiable trust. This toolkit offers pragmatic structures for activating convergence in workflows, platforms, and governance.

Each framework in this section bridges intelligence and enforceability—helping institutions answer not only "What should we do?" but also "Can we prove what we did?"

Framework 1: Convergence Readiness Grid

The Readiness Grid helps leaders pinpoint high-friction, high-value workflows where convergence delivers tangible ROI. These are not abstract opportunities—they are operational bottlenecks where decisions are slow, reconciliation is costly, and accountability is fragmented.

By examining five core dimensions—workflow type, friction points, agentic opportunity, blockchain opportunity, and convergence potential—teams can map where to begin. For instance, a liquidity transfer delayed by cut-off windows may benefit from agentic detection combined with programmable settlement, while a KYC onboarding process constrained by document checks could benefit from verifiable credentials and autonomous verification.

This grid doesn't just identify use cases; it guides pilot selection by highlighting where value is clear, and dependency on legacy infrastructure is low. It invites teams to focus where convergence isn't speculative—it's solvable.

Convergence Readiness Grid (Excerpt)

Work-flow	Current Friction	Agentic Opportunity	Block-chain Opportunity	Convergence Potential
Cross--border Liquidity	Cut-off times, reconciliation delays	Fore-casting, exception detection	Tokenized deposits, instant settlement	High
Client Onboarding	Manual KYC reviews, document fatigue	Credential verifica-tion, triage	Verifiable credentials, shared attestations	Medium
Trade Finance	Multi-party coordination, delays	Shipment tracking, risk scoring	Smart contracts for conditional collateral	High
FX Hedging	Lagged execution, manual approvals	Anomaly detection, policy alignment	On-chain policy enforce-ment	Medium

Framework 2: Reasoning + Verification Trail Map

As agents begin to recommend and trigger financial actions, and programmable contracts begin to execute them, the integrity of the end-to-end process depends on traceability. The Reasoning + Verification Trail Map ensures that every recommendation made by an AI agent and every action executed on a blockchain is logged, explainable, and auditable—not just internally, but to regulators and external stakeholders.

This framework creates dual visibility: a reasoning trail capturing the agent's logic, confidence score, and data inputs, and a verification trail documenting which smart contracts were invoked, what conditions were met, and which signatures authorized execution.

For example, when Lisa's liquidity agent detects a $50M shortfall in Singapore and proposes a reallocation from Frankfurt, the system doesn't just act. The agent logs its recommendation—"Forecasted stress level exceeds policy buffer by 18%, confidence 91%"—while the programmable rail logs the conditions validated and approvals confirmed. Lisa's explainability console links both logs in one interface, ensuring she, her compliance officer, and regulators all see the same end-to-end trail.

Implementing this trail map means standardizing formats across agent logs and smart contract metadata, aligning language between AI teams and blockchain engineers, and designing dashboards for real-time monitoring and retrospective audits. The goal is not just visibility—it's accountability at machine speed.

Reasoning + Verification Trail Map

Component	Details Captured
Agent Recommendation	"Shift $25M surplus from Frankfurt to Singapore. Confidence: 91%."
Policy Layer	Basel liquidity thresholds, dual authorization requirement
Smart Contract Execution	Contract ID #TX9242, validated inputs, approvals recorded on-chain
Audit Access	Lisa views reasoning in console; compliance accesses execution ledger

Framework 3: Fusion Team Charter

Convergence cannot be owned by a single department. When agentic systems begin triggering blockchain-based execution, the boundaries between product, risk, compliance, and technology dissolve. The Fusion Team Charter provides a structured model for cross-functional collaboration—where intelligence meets infrastructure, and governance is embedded from the start.

At its core is the Agentic-Blockchain Steward: a new institutional role responsible for overseeing the interaction between AI agents and programmable rails. This steward ensures that logic loops are consistent, overrides are captured, and execution conforms to pre-set thresholds. Around them, a fusion team forms—bringing together compliance officers, treasury leads, smart contract engineers, and system architects.

Weekly syncs ensure that operational issues (latency, overrides, contract errors) are addressed quickly. Monthly governance reviews identify pattern shifts, anomalies, or risks that require policy adjustment. When a divergence occurs—say, an agent recommends a trade but the contract fails due to a policy mismatch—the escalation protocol defines who intervenes, how decisions are logged, and what gets updated.

This charter is not a static document—it is a living agreement. As convergence expands, so does the team's mandate. The goal is not just alignment—it's resilience in complexity.

Framework 4: Infrastructure Interoperability Matrix

As institutions explore programmable finance, one risk looms large: fragmentation. With agents operating across legacy systems, private ledgers, and emerging public networks, interoperability becomes essential—not just for technical compatibility, but for strategic flexibility. The Infrastructure Interoperability Matrix offers a design lens for ensuring that agentic intelligence can operate across diverse infrastructures without getting locked into a single stack.

This framework spans four layers:

- **Data Layer**: Agents must ingest structured and unstructured data across systems. APIs, event streams, and data schemas need normalization. Without this, intelligence is blind.
- **Execution Layer**: Smart contracts differ across blockchains. Execution environments must be abstracted—using orchestration middleware or modular wrappers—so agents can deploy intent across any programmable rail.
- **Identity Layer**: Agents must verify who they're dealing with. Whether through legacy KYC systems, verifiable credentials, or decentralized identity networks, credential alignment is critical.
- **Governance Layer**: Overrides, audit trails, and compliance engines must work across systems. Governance tooling needs to be portable, with policies enforced regardless of rail or ledger.

Lisa's agents demonstrate this matrix in motion. On Monday, they settle liquidity using tokenized deposits on a private ledger. On Tuesday, they interact with a public stablecoin network. On Wednesday, they route through Fedwire. In each case, the reasoning is consistent—even when the rail changes. This is convergence with optionality.

Designing for interoperability future-proofs institutional strategy. It ensures that the infrastructure does not dictate the institution's intent—but that intelligence flows where it's needed, governed and intact.

Framework 5: Convergence Metrics Dashboard

When decisions are made by agents and executed through programmable infrastructure, measurement is more than a performance tool—it becomes the anchor of trust. The Convergence Metrics Dashboard offers a cross-domain lens to track not only how well systems perform, but how reliably they align with institutional policy, compliance expectations, and client experience.

This dashboard spans five key dimensions:
- **Time to Decision (AI Layer)**: How quickly do agents detect signals, evaluate scenarios, and surface recommendations? Lag here signals model drift, data latency, or incomplete context.
- **Time to Settlement (Blockchain Layer)**: Once a decision is made, how long does it take to execute on-chain? This includes contract validation, compliance checks, and finality.
- **Override Rate**: How often are agentic decisions halted, amended, or reversed by human reviewers? A spike could indicate

overreach, unclear thresholds, or trust erosion.

- **Audit Log Completeness**: Do all actions—recommendations, contract executions, approvals—generate traceable logs? Completeness ensures post-incident review and regulatory defensibility.
- **Regulatory SLA Compliance**: Are programmable decisions adhering to internal control standards and external policy mandates? This measures alignment with frameworks like MiFID II, Basel III, or AML directives.

Lisa's team integrates these metrics directly into operational dashboards. When a treasury agent reallocates $50M via tokenized deposits, both the decision timestamp and settlement log are recorded. Overrides trigger alerts. Audit logs are piped to compliance review interfaces. Over time, these metrics enable not just system optimization but institutional learning.

Metrics don't just describe what happened—they guide what should happen next. In convergence, they become both compass and ledger.

Convergence Toolkit Summary

Framework	Purpose	Primary Use Case	Key Roles
Convergence Readiness Grid	Identify high-friction, high-value pilot workflows	Liquidity, KYC, trade finance	Strategy leads, Product owners
Reasoning + Verification Trail	Dual-log agent and blockchain execution	Treasury reallocations, onboarding checks	Compliance, AI leads, Risk
Fusion Team Charter	Define cross-functional convergence governance	Scaling pilots, managing escalations	Agentic-Blockchain Steward, Ops leads
Infrastructure Interoperability	Ensure seamless agent activity across all rails	Switching between legacy and programmable	Tech architects, Smart contract teams
Convergence Metrics Dashboard	Measure performance, alignment, and auditability	Quarterly reviews, regulator briefings	Board, Audit, Governance teams

From Toolset to Transformation

As institutions transition into the agentic era, frameworks alone are not enough. What determines success is how deliberately these tools are applied, who owns them, how they're measured, and whether they evolve alongside the systems they govern. These models are designed not as fixed templates but as activation points. They invite co--creation, iteration, and reflection across functions.

In practice, the most powerful outcomes emerge when strategy, operations, and technology converge on a shared design language. The readiness checklists, journey canvases, and governance layers outlined here offer more than structure, they offer a way to align intent with execution, autonomy with accountability.

Use this appendix as a working playbook. Mark it up. Share it with teams. Return to it as agents scale across your business. Because the future of banking won't be shaped by code alone, but by how well we orchestrate intelligence, talent, and trust into the systems we build.

CONCLUSION

The future doesn't arrive all at once. It emerges in signals, small, persistent, undeniable. This book has traced those signals: the rise of agents as collaborators rather than mere features; systems that learn, act, and evolve; and the transformation of banking and decision-making into something more intelligent, adaptive, and aligned. Institutions are beginning to think, sense, and decide with a fluency that feels less like machinery and more like intelligence.

Banking has always advanced in waves. Electronic trading compressed markets into milliseconds, changing the physics of finance itself. ATMs and cards redefined convenience and accessibility, teaching clients to expect banking wherever they were, whenever they needed it. The platform era unified fragmented services under a single digital roof, scaling reach and efficiency beyond what branch networks could ever achieve. Each wave did more than improve processes; it redefined client expectations, reshaped regulator priorities, and forced institutions to evolve or fall behind.

Yet what we are witnessing today is categorically different. Platforms, for all their power, were still designed to serve human decision-makers. They centralized data and standardized workflows, but the final leap, the synthesis of signals into judgment, was still left to people. Relationship managers logged into multiple systems before client meetings, compliance officers scrolled through hundreds of alerts to identify a single genuine risk, and treasurers pored over spreadsheets long after markets had moved. Platforms accelerated access, but the work of sense-making remained human.

That era is fading. Intelligence is no longer an accessory to the institution, it is woven into its operations. Agents don't simply extend platforms; they transform them into partners. They generate reasoning trails, anticipate outcomes, and propose actions in real time. They orchestrate workflows across systems, surfaces, and silos. In doing so, they shift the cognitive load from human shoulders to shared intelligence, freeing people to concentrate on judgment, empathy, creativity, and strategy, the things only people can uniquely bring.

This shift is not just technological progress. It is a redefinition of institutional capacity. Decision-making becomes continuous rather than episodic. Governance becomes embedded rather than reactive. Trust is earned not by opacity or tradition but by explainability and transparency. The question for leaders is no longer whether banks will embrace these capabilities but how they will do so, with clarity of intent, with responsibility, and with foresight.

We have explored this shift through arcs of transformation. From dashboards to decisions: where once dashboards presented static data and left interpretation to the user, agentic systems now bridge the gap, delivering reasoning, surfacing anomalies, and proposing actions with confidence scores attached. Hours of analysis collapse into moments of decision-ready intelligence.

From channels to collaboration: where digital channels once connected institutions to clients, they now evolve into conversational environments where agents, clients, and bankers engage together in real time. Clients no longer navigate interfaces alone; they are guided by intelligent copilots that anticipate needs, flag risks, and propose opportunities before the human even asks.

From oversight to orchestration: where oversight once meant backward-looking checks after processes had ended, orchestration now coordinates humans, agents, and systems in real time. Boundaries are respected automatically, exceptions are escalated intelligently, and conflicts are resolved before they materialize into risk.

And these are only the beginning. The deeper horizon includes the shift from platforms to partners, where systems cease to be tools that must be driven by humans and instead become teammates, taking responsibility within defined guardrails while preserving accountability. From data as input to data as dialogue, where information ceases to be a static resource and instead becomes an active, conversational element of decision-making, constantly updating as new signals arrive. From risk as compliance to risk as continuous alignment, where governance ceases to be retrospective and instead becomes a dynamic, living process. And from efficiency as an end-state to adaptability as a true competitive advantage, where composability and orchestration allow institutions to thrive in volatility, not just survive it.

These are not abstractions. They are practical realities already unfolding. When Lisa's treasury avoided emergency borrowing because agents connected a typhoon alert to outstanding receivables, that was dashboards becoming decisions. When Ravi's team resolved a compliance conflict mid-trade instead of post-audit, that was oversight becoming orchestration. When a client co-pilot turned fragmented data into a clear proposal before a meeting, that was data becoming dialogue. These examples are signals of a structural transformation: early adopters are not just faster, they are fundamentally different.

Transformation in banking has never been the product of consensus. It has always begun with a few leaders who could see faint signals before they became undeniable. The first to embrace electronic trading reshaped capital markets. The pioneers of mobile banking redefined customer expectations across continents. The architects of platform ecosystems set new standards for scale and reach. None of these leaders were simply implementing tools; they were reshaping intent, vision, and the very definition of what a bank could be.

The rise of agentic systems now raises the stakes further. For the first time, intelligence itself is becoming part of the institution's fabric. Decisions are not merely represented in dashboards or reports; they are embedded in code, orchestrated in real time, and amplified through autonomous collaboration. This brings extraordinary opportunity, but also extraordinary responsibility. Because when intelligence becomes infrastructure, leadership becomes stewardship.

The question facing today's boards and executive teams is not whether to adopt AI agents, it is how to govern them. Regulators are recalibrating around explainability, fairness, and systemic resilience.

Clients are demanding personalization delivered with transparency and accountability. Teams want clarity about how their human judgment integrates with algorithmic reasoning. And societies at large expect that intelligent banks will reinforce, not erode, stability, inclusion, and trust.

Agentic leadership is therefore not a technical project but a boardroom mandate and a societal obligation. Leaders must hold themselves accountable not just for shareholder returns but for the intent embedded in their systems, for the transparency of their reasoning, and for the resilience of their institutions under stress. Just as past generations of banking leaders were stewards of capital and solvency, today's leaders must be stewards of intelligence, embedding explainability as deeply as efficiency, composability as deeply as scalability, governance as deeply as growth.

This stewardship demands courage in ambiguity, clarity in complexity, and conviction in purpose. It requires recognizing that deploying agentic systems is not a one-time project but an ongoing dialogue: between institutions and regulators, between systems and users, between intelligence and intent. It requires leaders to embrace humility, that no model is permanent, no trust is guaranteed, and foresight, that these systems must be built to adapt across decades, not just quarters.

If the past decade was about digitization and platforms, the next will be about cognition and collaboration. The institutions that thrive will not be the ones that simply adopt agents, but those that build living, adaptive systems, systems that learn continuously, govern transparently, and align seamlessly with human purpose. The fully agentic bank will not feel like a bank that has added intelligence. It will feel like an intelligence that carries out the functions of a bank.

Picture that horizon. Liquidity managed dynamically across time zones, with funding decisions executed preemptively rather than reactively. Compliance conducted as a live dialogue with regulators, with every decision fully auditable at the moment it is made. Client interactions transformed into conversations where needs are anticipated before they are expressed. Risk models that not only protect balance sheets but also shape strategy, guiding capital toward its safest and highest use.

In this horizon, trust scaffolds and governance meshes are not optional, they are the new competitive edge. Institutions will not distinguish themselves by how much intelligence they deploy but by how responsibly they steward it. Composability will separate resilience from rigidity, enabling institutions to adapt as markets shift, regulations evolve, and client expectations rise. Agentic governance will determine whether intelligence amplifies institutional purpose, or undermines it.

This journey has no finish line. It will be defined by continuous learning loops where every override, every escalation, every failure becomes input for improvement. It will be shaped by humility that acknowledges impermanence, and foresight that builds systems capable of generational adaptation.

Most importantly, the agentic bank is not merely a financial innovation. It is a societal one. The ways in which intelligence is embedded in our systems will define not only efficiency and profitability, but fairness, accessibility, and resilience across the communities banks serve. Banking has always been an act of trust at scale. In the agentic era, that trust will be redefined by how intelligently, and how responsibly, we orchestrate intelligence, talent, and values together.

And so the question for every leader is inescapable: What kind of institution are we becoming? The answer will not be written in memos or strategy decks but encoded in the systems we build, in the agents we authorize, and in the governance we enforce. The agentic bank is no longer an idea on the horizon; it is here, shaping treasury flows, compliance frameworks, and client interactions today. The choice is whether to lead this transformation deliberately, with clarity and courage, or to inherit it passively, on terms defined by competitors and constraints.

The future of finance will not be defined by code alone but by how courageously we weave intelligence, human judgment, and institutional purpose into the systems that carry us forward. The signals are already here. The horizon is clear. The only question is who among us will have the courage to lead.

GLOSSARY OF TERMS

T his glossary is intended to clarify the foundational terms, acronyms, and concepts referenced throughout *The Agentic Bank*. It is designed to assist executives, board members, and financial professionals in navigating the language of agentic systems and AI transformation.

Core Agentic & AI Concepts

Agentic System
A system composed of autonomous agents capable of perception, reasoning, and action. These systems operate with a degree of independence and are adaptable to goals and context, representing a shift from static tools to dynamic collaborators.

AI (Artificial Intelligence)
The field of computer science focused on building systems that can perform tasks requiring human-like cognition, such as decision-making, problem-solving, and language understanding.

AI Agent
An autonomous software program that performs tasks on behalf of users or systems. In finance, these agents can initiate actions, interpret data, and collaborate with humans or other agents across domains.

LLM (Large Language Model)
An AI model trained on vast datasets to understand and generate human language. LLMs form the core intelligence in many agentic systems and can be fine-tuned or augmented for enterprise use.

RAG (Retrieval-Augmented Generation)

A hybrid AI method where an LLM retrieves relevant documents or data before generating a response. RAG grounds answers in facts and enterprise-specific knowledge.

RLHF (Reinforcement Learning from Human Feedback)

A training method where human preferences are used to guide model behavior. Essential for aligning LLM outputs with institutional tone, policy, and objectives.

Co-Pilot / Digital Assistant

Task-specific AI interfaces that support users by summarizing, generating, or recommending actions within applications. Often embedded in platforms like Microsoft 365 or Salesforce.

Memory System (Agentic Memory)

An agent's ability to retain and recall contextual information over time. Enables personalization, situational awareness, and long-term decision continuity.

Enterprise Architecture and Data

ERP (Enterprise Resource Planning)
Integrated enterprise systems, such as SAP or Oracle, that manage finance, operations, procurement, and supply chain workflows. In agentic banking, ERP data feeds (accounts payable, receivable, settlement schedules) are critical inputs for liquidity agents, intraday forecasting, and working capital optimization.

API (Application Programming Interface)
A standardized method for software applications to communicate and share data. Essential for integrating agents with enterprise systems.

Composability (Data/System)
A design principle where systems and datasets are modular, interoperable, and easily reassembled to fit evolving workflows or goals.

SWIFT gpi (Global Payments Innovation)
A cross-border payments standard developed by SWIFT that enables faster, more transparent, and trackable international transactions. For agentic banking, gpi feeds provide real-time visibility into payment flows and settlement confirmations.

Fedwire

The U.S. Federal Reserve's real-time gross settlement system for large-value transfers. Agentic treasury systems connect directly to Fedwire streams to balance intraday liquidity, monitor high-value settlements, and prevent overdrafts.

Event Stream Processing

A real-time data architecture that continuously ingests and analyzes event streams (e.g., Kafka, Pulsar). Forms the perception layer of agentic systems by enabling continuous monitoring of payments, markets, and operations.

UX (User Experience)

The holistic experience of interacting with a digital product or system, including how intuitive, efficient, and effective it is.

Treasury and Risk

T+1 (Transaction Plus One Day)

A financial settlement convention where a transaction is finalized one business day after the trade date. Relevant to liquidity and treasury operations.

FX (Foreign Exchange)

The global market for trading currencies. FX volatility is a key trigger in many treasury agent workflows.

Intraday Liquidity

The monitoring and management of payment flows within a single business day. Agentic systems enable continuous liquidity balancing across geographies and currencies.

Funding Spread

The difference between a bank's borrowing cost and a benchmark rate. Treasury agents monitor spreads in real time, dynamically adjusting funding strategies to minimize cost of capital.

Hedging Ratio

The proportion of an exposure that is protected through hedging instruments. Risk agents calculate and rebalance hedging ratios continuously as market conditions evolve.

LCR (Liquidity Coverage Ratio)

A Basel III metric requiring banks to hold sufficient high-quality liquid assets (HQLA) to cover net cash outflows over 30 days. Agentic liquidity agents track LCR continuously, adjusting buffers in real time.

NSFR (Net Stable Funding Ratio)
A Basel III requirement ensuring banks maintain a stable funding structure over a one-year horizon. Agentic systems optimize funding strategies to balance short-term liquidity with long-term stability.

Stress Testing
The process of simulating extreme or adverse scenarios to test financial resilience. Agentic systems transform stress testing from periodic exercises to continuous, real-time simulations.

ICAAP (Internal Capital Adequacy Assessment Process)
A regulatory framework where banks assess their internal capital requirements under various stress conditions. Agentic capital strategy agents enhance ICAAP with live scenario modeling.

Digital Twin (Finance)
A virtual replica of a financial system, portfolio, or balance sheet used for real-time simulations. Supports treasury optimization, risk testing, and capital planning.

Governance and Oversight

Governance Mesh
A framework of controls, rules, audit trails, and escalation protocols that supervises AI agents. It ensures compliance, safety, and ethical alignment in dynamic environments.

Trust Scaffold
The layered infrastructure, including explainability, oversight, and human override, that builds institutional confidence in agentic systems.

HITL (Human-in-the-Loop)
A model design where human oversight is integrated at critical decision points, ensuring judgment, accountability, and alignment in agentic operations.

Kill Switch
A built-in control that allows institutions to halt or disable agent activity immediately in case of malfunction, misalignment, or systemic risk. An essential safeguard for operational resilience.

Bias Mitigation
The set of methods used to detect, monitor, and reduce unfair or discriminatory outcomes

in AI systems. Critical for maintaining trust and regulatory compliance in agentic decision-making.

Red Teaming (AI)

A governance practice where adversarial tests, stress cases, or simulated attacks are applied to agentic systems. Ensures robustness, security, and ethical alignment under real-world conditions.

Explainability by Design

The principle of embedding transparency and reasoning narration directly into agentic system architecture rather than treating it as an afterthought.

Model Risk Management (MRM)

The discipline of validating, monitoring, and controlling risks associated with AI/ML models. A core governance requirement for regulated financial institutions.

Regulatory and Compliance

KYC (Know Your Customer)

A compliance process that verifies the identity and risk profile of a client, a frequent domain of automation and AI-driven due diligence.

AML (Anti-Money Laundering)
Regulatory controls and systems that detect and prevent illicit financial activity. Agentic systems can support real-time monitoring and escalation.

MiFID (Markets in Financial Instruments Directive)
An EU regulatory framework that governs investment services and activities. AI systems in finance must align with such frameworks.

GDPR (General Data Protection Regulation)
The European Union's data privacy law. Governs how personal data is collected, stored, and used, with direct implications for AI governance.

Basel III
A global regulatory standard for bank capital adequacy, stress testing, and liquidity risk. Agentic systems must respect constraints defined by Basel rules.

CCAR (Comprehensive Capital Analysis and Review)
A U.S. regulatory framework requiring banks to conduct rigorous stress testing of capital adequacy under adverse scenarios. Agentic systems transform CCAR from an annual submission into a continuous, automated process.

DORA (Digital Operational Resilience Act)
An EU regulation establishing ICT risk management standards for financial institutions. Agentic oversight systems align with DORA by continuously monitoring operational resilience and third-party dependencies.

PSD2 (Payment Services Directive 2)
An EU regulation mandating secure, open access to banking data through APIs. Provides the regulatory foundation for agentic payments, account aggregation, and embedded financial services.

ESG (Environmental, Social, and Governance)
A framework for evaluating the sustainability and ethical impact of an institution's operations and investments. In agentic banking, ESG agents continuously monitor portfolios, supply chains, and operations to ensure compliance and align with stakeholder expectations.

CBDC (Central Bank Digital Currency)
A digital form of a nation's fiat currency, issued and regulated by its central bank. CBDCs can enable programmable payments, real-time settlement, and regulatory oversight, while retaining sovereign control.

Stablecoin
A digital currency designed to maintain a stable value, typically pegged to fiat currencies like the USD or EUR. Stablecoins are increasingly used for cross-border payments, intraday liquidity, and programmable settlements.

Asset Tokenization
The conversion of real-world or financial assets into digital tokens on a blockchain. These tokens carry embedded logic such as eligibility criteria, risk parameters, and settlement conditions, enabling automated asset flows.

Programmable Rail / Programmable Finance
A financial infrastructure layer where assets or money carry embedded logic—allowing for conditional execution, real-time compliance checks, and cryptographic auditability. Supports automation of complex financial workflows.

Digital Identity / Verifiable Credential
Cryptographically secure, machine-readable credentials that verify the identity or status of a person, institution, or asset. These credentials enable instant onboarding, risk classification, and permissioned access across systems.

Convergence (AI + Blockchain)

The integration of intelligent agents (AI) with programmable execution environments (blockchain), allowing institutions to align decision-making speed with enforceable, auditable execution. A foundational design principle in agentic banking.

Geographic Terms

EMEA (Europe, the Middle East, and Africa)

A geographic business region commonly referenced in financial and corporate strategy. Often used to describe operations or regulatory environments specific to these areas.

LATAM (Latin America)

A regional designation that includes South and Central America, commonly referenced in the context of market segmentation, regulatory frameworks, and regional growth strategies.

APAC (Asia-Pacific)

A business region covering East Asia, South Asia, Southeast Asia, and Oceania. Critical for understanding regional dynamics in banking and technology adoption.

ABOUT THE AUTHOR

Driss Temsamani is a global thought leader in institutional finance, digital transformation, tokenization, and AI strategy. With more than three decades of experience in banking leadership, he has helped multinational institutions adapt to disruptive technologies while staying grounded in business impact.

He has led strategic initiatives across treasury and finance, laying the foundation for what he calls "agentic institutions": intelligent organizations that don't just automate, but collaborate.

A frequent keynote speaker at global finance and technology forums, including economic conferences, industry councils, and fintech summits, Driss bridges systems thinking, policy, and design with a deep commitment to delivering measurable value for clients and institutions alike.

He also advises central banks and regulators on how to responsibly integrate blockchain and AI into financial systems at scale. Driss believes the future of finance is not just digital, it's intelligent, human-centered, and agentic.

Contact

Driss Temsamani welcomes dialogue with readers interested in the future of banking, digital transformation, and the role of intelligent systems in finance.

For inquiries please connect through the following email: info@drisstemsamani.com

www.TheAgenticBank.ai

Instagram: @theagenticbank

Youtube: @TheAgenticBank

www.ingramcontent.com/pod-product-compliance
Lightning Source LLC
Chambersburg PA
CBHW031805190326
41518CB00006B/209